Building an On Demand Computing Environment with IBM

Other Items of Interest

More IBM Books

- *Exploring IBM Technology, Products and Services*
- *Exploring IBM e-business Software*
- *Exploring IBM **@server** pSeries*
- *Exploring IBM **@server** iSeries*
- *Exploring IBM **@server** xSeries*
- *Exploring IBM **@server** zSeries*
- and many more…

Top e-business Books

- *101 Ways to Promote Your Web Site*
- *Business-to-Business Internet Marketing*
- *Marketing on the Internet*
- and many more…

Special Offers

From IBM and other "*Exploring IBM*" team members

Building an On Demand Computing Environment with IBM

How to Optimize Your Current Infrastructure for Today and Tomorrow

by Jim Hoskins

(version 1.0p)

MAXIMUM PRESS
605 Silverthorn Road
Gulf Breeze, FL 32561
(850) 934-0819
www.maxpress.com

Notices

Production Manager: Gina Cooke

Cover Designer: Lauren Smith

Copyeditor: Andy Potter

Proofreader: Jacquie Wallace

Manager of Finance/Administration: Joyce Reedy

This publication is designed to provide accurate and authoritative information in regard to the subject matter covered. It is sold with the understanding that the publisher is not engaged in rendering professional services. If legal, accounting, medical, psychological, or any other expert assistance is required, the services of a competent professional person should be sought. ADAPTED FROM A DECLARATION OF PRINCIPLES OF A JOINT COMMITTEE OF THE AMERICAN BAR ASSOCIATION AND PUBLISHERS.

This report was sponsored by IBM. This report utilized information provided by IBM and other companies including publicly available data. This report represents Maximum Press' view point and does not necessarily represent IBM's position on these issues.

Library of Congress Cataloging-in-Publication Data

Hoskins, Jim.
Building an on demand computing environment with IBM: how to optimize your current IBM infrastructure for today and tomorrow / Jim Hoskins.— 1st ed.
p. cm.
ISBN 1-931644-11-X (pbk.)
1. Computers. 2. Computer software. 3. Computer systems. 4. Business—Data processing. 5. IBM computers. I. Title.
QA76.H668 2003
004.165—dc22

2003018281

Acknowledgments

Many people gave assistance in preparation of this ebook. Some provided information concerning their product area of expertise. Others reviewed the manuscript and provided helpful comments. To all of those who assisted... THANK YOU!!

Disclaimer

The purchase of computer software or hardware is an important and costly business decision. While the author and publisher of this ebook have made reasonable efforts to ensure the accuracy and timeliness of the information contained herein, the author and publisher assume no liability with respect to loss or damage caused or alleged to be caused by reliance on any information contained herein and disclaim any and all warranties, expressed or implied, as to the accuracy or reliability of said information.

This book is not intended to replace the manufacturer's product documentation or personnel in determining the specifications and capabilities of the products mentioned in this book. The manufacturer's product documentation should always be consulted, as the specifications and capabilities of computer hardware and software products are subject to frequent modification. The reader is solely responsible for the choice of computer hardware and software. All configurations and applications of computer hardware and software should be reviewed with the manufacturer's representatives prior to choosing or using any computer hardware and software.

Trademarks

Table of Contents

Introduction

About This MaxFacts™ Guidebook

IBM has embarked on a sweeping, company-wide strategy called "e-business on demand" that consists of three elements: Business Transformation, Operating Environment, and Flexible Financial and Delivery Methods. This *MaxFacts™ Guidebook* starts with an overall look at the on demand strategy and what it means to businesses today and tomorrow. It will then focus in on the "Operating Environment" element of that strategy to help you see how to leverage your current information technology (IT) investment and gain the benefits associated with becoming an on demand business. Finally, we will take a look at the roadmaps that will guide the future of on demand computing.

About the "More On The Web" Boxes

Throughout this *MaxFacts™ Guidebook* you will see inset boxes labeled "More On The Web." These boxes tell you about some of the links that are provided on the companion Web site for this book. To see how to access these links and the rest of the companion Web site resources, see the "Your 'Members Only' Web Site" section below. The URLs for the links are also listed in Appendix A.

Your "Members Only" Web Site

The on demand world changes every day. That's why there is a companion Web site associated with this book. On the site you will find the latest on demand news, links to expanded information referenced in the "More On The Web" boxes found in this book, and other related resources. However, you have to be a member of the "Insiders Club" to gain access to this site. When you purchased this book, you automatically became a member (in fact, that's the only way to join), so you now have full privileges.

To get into the "Members Only" section of the companion Web site, go to the Maximum Press Web site (*www.maxpress.com*) and follow the links to the *Building an On Demand Computing Environment with IBM* companion Web site. When you try to enter, you will be asked for a user ID and password. Type in the following:

- For your user ID, enter: *ondemandoe*
- For your password, enter: *smoky*

You will then be granted full access to the "Members Only" area. Visit the site often and enjoy the updates and resources with our compliments—and thanks again for buying the book. We ask that you not share the user ID and password for this site with anyone else.

Reader Feedback

We welcome your feedback on any aspect of this publication, so please e-mail us at *moreinfo@maxpress.com*. To see our full line of Exploring IBM books, we invite you to visit our Web site at *www.maxpress.com*.

More on the Web

- Maximum Press Web site

(see page x)

From all of us at Maximum Press, thank you for your interest in our *MaxFacts*™ *Guidebooks*.

CHAPTER 1

The On Demand Journey

In this chapter, we will take an overall look at IBM's company-wide vision for the future of business and information technology, namely, "e-business on demand." This will provide an overall context for our subsequent discussions, which will focus on the "operating environment" component of the on demand strategy.

What Is An On Demand Business?

IBM has been laser focused on a strategy called e-business on demand (or simply on demand) ever since its introduction in October of 2002. You can already see the results of this focus in many of today's IBM products and services. And the $10 billion IBM is committing to the on demand philosophy means that this strategy will increasingly manifest itself in all business consulting activities, computer hardware, software, and IT services over time. Many companies in many different industries have already started on demand initiatives.

At its core, on demand refers to the ability of a business to effectively respond to change. In the words of IBM Chairman and CEO Sam Palmisano, an on demand enterprise is one "...whose business processes-integrated end-to-end across the company and with key partners, suppliers and customers can respond with flexibility and speed to any customer demand, market opportunity, or external threat." While the typical business organizational structures, processes, and underlying infrastructures in place today meet current needs (to a varying degree), they are not prepared to efficiently support a highly dynamic, responsive, and integrated business environment—which is exactly where business is headed.

IBM will be the first to tell you that they did not invent the on demand concept. Rather, it is an outgrowth of what the business community told IBM they needed to be successful in today's fast changing world, namely, the ability to be more dynamic. And this is a burning desire within businesses of all sizes and in all industries. IBM's competitors are also beginning to forward concepts similar to those embodied in the IBM on demand vision. However, no other company has the breadth of products, services (both business and technical), and experience being offered by IBM. Timing is everything… and this enviable position comes at a time when businesses are in need of solutions with broader scope than ever before.

Any meaningful discussion of the on demand concept must start at the business level rather than with technology. That is, the business goals must be the driving force behind the transformation to an on demand model. So let's start by forgetting about technology for a moment and focusing on the four attributes of an on demand business. According to IBM, an on demand business must be:

Responsive

An on demand business has the ability to sense and respond in real time to a dynamic marketplace. Doing this effectively requires a clear and integrated view of customers, employees, suppliers, partners, and competitors.

Variable

An on demand business has flexible and adaptive cost structures and business processes. This requires a migration from fixed cost structures to variable cost structures that can scale with business volume, thereby reducing risk, improving productivity, and optimizing business performance.

Focused

An on demand business concentrates on its core competencies and the value it provides to its customers. It focuses on constantly improving in ways that help differentiate the business from its competitors. Distractions are avoided by building strategic relationships with qualified business partners that manage selected tasks ranging from manufacturing, logistics, and fulfillment to HR and financial operations.

Resilient

An on demand business is prepared to detect and respond to unexpected threats or changes in the marketplace. This readiness is achieved through the implementation of a flexible operating environment that continuously evolves toward ever-improving availability, security, and privacy.

Becoming an On Demand Business

In this section we will take at look at how you go about gathering the parts of the on demand puzzle.

A Journey, Not a Destination

If it came in a box, everyone would have it. There is no "one thing" you can go and buy, no "single action" you can take to become an on demand business. Rather, the path to on demand is an evolutionary trail. So the first principle to keep in mind as you plan your migration toward becoming an on demand business is that it is an ongoing journey, not a destination. The good news is, you achieve new business benefits at every step along the on demand path. So the rewards accrue all during the journey, not just at some distant destination.

MORE ON THE WEB

- Webcast: Sam Palmisano presents on demand
- On demand introductory information
- Paper: Living in an on demand world

(see page x)

As depicted in Figure 1.1, IBM describes three elements that are part of the on demand journey: Business Transformation, Operating Environment, Flexible Financial and Delivery Methods. Let's take a closer look at each.

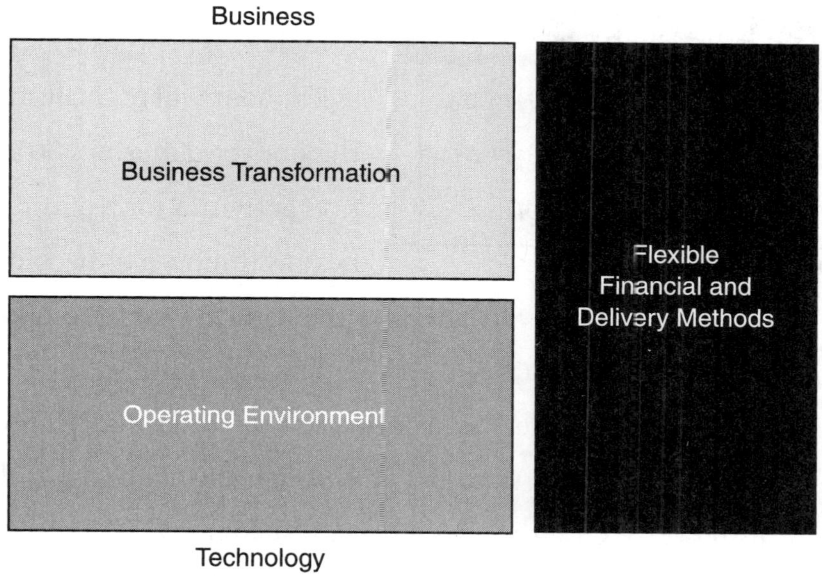

Figure 1.1. The three elements of the on demand journey.

Business Transformation

The on demand journey begins with a focus on the business as a whole. The "Business Transformation" (BT) element of the on demand strategy provides the methodology and tools necessary for a thorough analysis of the current situation followed by transformation planning and implementation. Business transformation is about fundamentally improving the organizational structures, processes, and competitive standing of a business.

Depending on the situation, BT typically starts with an on demand customer assessment ranging from a two-day workshop to a more

More on the Web

- Business Transformation Overview
- IBM Business Consulting Services
- Integrated Industry Solutions

(see page x)

complex eight-week analysis. This assessment will identify and quantify the impact of business transformation activities for a particular business as it moves to becoming an on demand business. Figure 1.2 depicts the basic BT adoption process a business will follow as it begins its on demand journey.

To support its business transformation offerings, IBM is leveraging the deep business skills they gained through the acquisition of the PwC Consulting (PwCC) group in October of 2002. PwCC merged with an

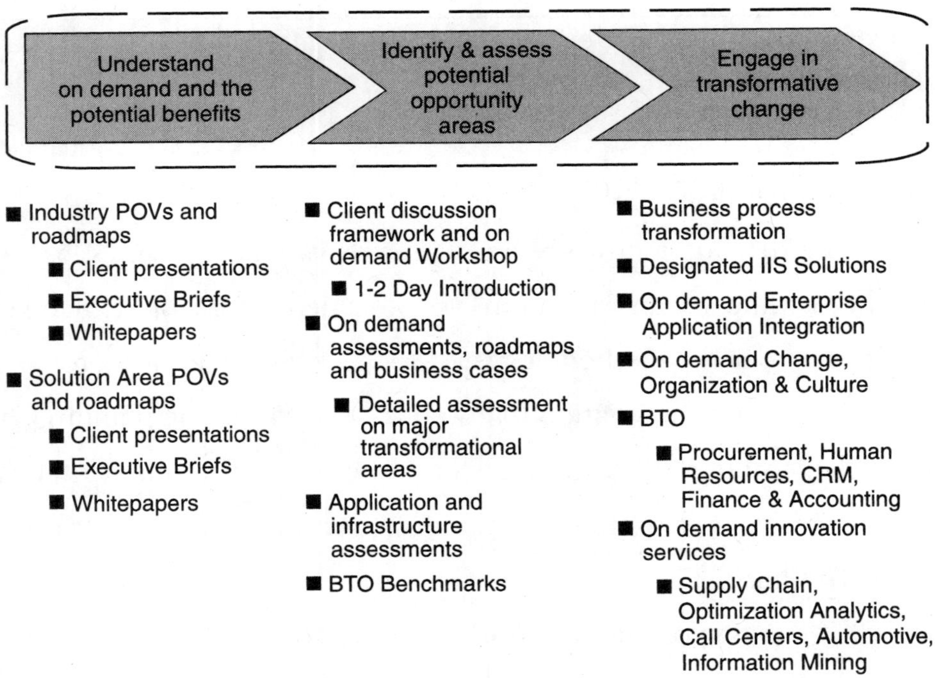

Figure 1.2. Business transformation adoption process.

arm of IBM Global Services to become IBM Business Consulting Services (BCS). BCS now comprises 60,000 employees with business expertise and experience in 18 different industries.

Operating Environment

At its core, the on demand strategy refers to a business's need to respond to change both quickly and effectively. To support this need, the business must have a flexible computing infrastructure (hardware, software, and services all working together). This is what IBM calls an "on demand operating environment." More specifically, IBM states that an on demand operating environment is "...an end-to-end enabling IT infrastructure that can allow a business to execute IT operations that align with its business strategy. An IT infrastructure enables a business to be more responsive, to focus on core competencies, to benefit from variable cost structures and to be resilient to external threats." By having such an operating environment, a business is free to spend more time and energy on the things that differentiate it from its competitors rather than on managing internal computer systems.

The computing infrastructures typically in use today are not yet prepared to support an on demand business model. So what does this mean? Well it doesn't mean that you need to throw everything away and start over from scratch. In fact, the on demand strategy is being deployed in such a way as to leverage a business's existing investment in IBM hardware, software, and training. What it does mean is that every new purchase or project that comes under consideration should be carefully evaluated in the context of building an on demand operating environment.

In IBM language, this means you need to evolve your computing infrastructure over time such that it becomes increasingly integrated, open, virtualized, and autonomic. As depicted in Figure 1.3, these are the four key attributes that describe the operating environment necessary to support an on demand business. Let's take a quick look at each attribute.

Integrated

The "integrated" attribute refers to the facilitation of information flow. The free yet secure exchange of information between key business processes throughout the inner workings of a business as well as with

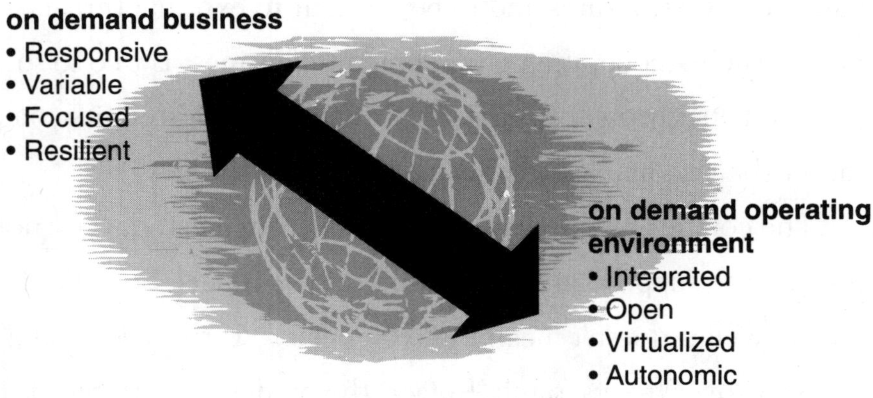

Figure 1.3. An on demand business must be supported by an underlying operating environment that is integrated, open, virtualized, and autonomic.

key suppliers and customers is one of the crown jewels of the on demand strategy. That's because integration breaks down the "silos" of information that create barriers to collaboration and allows business application programs to be more quickly deployed across organizational boundaries.

For maximum effectiveness, integration must occur at multiple levels. That is, information must be within reach of all authorized users (server and storage integration) and then properly interpreted by the various independent application programs that support core business processes (application program integration). So businesses should not allow the implementation of independent computer solutions (servers, storage, operating systems, middleware, and application programs) without giving careful thought to how these new solutions will be securely integrated (immediately or in the future) with the rest of the computing infrastructure.

Open

The days of locking into a specific vendor's proprietary computing architecture are gone. Today, a computing infrastructure needs the flexibility (in vendor choice, in information exchange, in application selection, etc.) that only comes when that infrastructure is built around open standards defined by vendor-neutral standards bodies—standards with names such as Java, Web services, XML, and Linux. Most businesses choose to construct heterogeneous computing infrastructures that will include more than one type of server/operating system... and for good reason. Adherence to open standards will protect these investments and enable these different types of systems to work together, or integrate, at a lower cost over time. Other benefits resulting from the adherence to open standards include leveraging investments/skills in existing heterogenous computing infrastructures, speed of deployment for new projects, and freedom of choice. For the same reasons, adherence is also important when selecting storage devices for use in an e-business infrastructure. The "open" attribute of an on demand operating environment refers to compliance with open standards over proprietary ones. The benefit offered by an open infrastructure is increased selection when choosing solutions to address the specific and dynamic business needs.

Virtualized

In a virtualized computing environment, what you get is more than what you see. That is, a virtualized computing infrastructure insulates the users and application programs from the detailed physical constraints of the infrastructure, resulting in both simplification and improved utilization. Virtualization allows underlying computing infrastructure components to be more easily managed, reconfigured, upgraded, and even repaired without disruption to users.

Virtualization also allows the computing infrastructure to pool disparate physical devices (e.g., servers, storage devices, middleware, etc.) and present a unified view of those resources to users and application pro-

MORE ON THE WEB

- The on demand operating environment
- IBM autonomic computing overview, news, library, etc.
- IBM Global Services

(see page x)

grams. These pools of resources can be shared and dynamically reallocated to users in concert with their changing needs—without disruption. Through this dynamic allocation of resources, a business can accomplish more work through a given computing infrastructure, resulting in better service and less wasted resources. The simplification and pooling of resources plays right into the hands of the on demand strategy.

Autonomic

"Autonomic" is a term IBM borrowed from the vernacular of the human central nervous system. The goal of autonomic computing is for the computing infrastructure to manage itself just as the central nervous system manages the human body—without our conscious effort. Making computer systems self-configuring, self-healing, self-optimizing, and self-protecting reduces the costs associated with systems management and unscheduled downtime. The more complex the computing system, the more important autonomic computing becomes.

These four attributes—integrated, open, virtualized, and autonomic—are the principles that IBM is using to guide the development of its entire line of infrastructure products and services. So increasingly you will see attributes enhanced in important IBM brands such as eServer, TotalStorage, InfoPrint, WebSphere, DB2, Lotus, Tivoli, and others (the subject of later chapters). This huge portfolio of hardware and software products, in conjunction with the IBM Global Services consulting arm, represents a clear competitive advantage for IBM. Many businesses are frustrated with having to integrate disparate technologies themselves, which plays to a major IBM strength—providing complete solutions rather than selling individual pieces to the on demand puzzle.

Flexible Financial and Delivery Methods

The third element in the IBM on demand strategy is called Flexible Financial and Delivery Methods. In short, this element offers new ways to acquire and manage the information technology needed to support an on demand business. Figure 1.4 depicts the different ways a business can acquire IT.

The horizontal axis of the graph represents the IT cost structure—how you pay for the IT you need. Traditionally, a business treats IT purchases as fixed costs. The resulting fixed cost and asset structure can hinder the variability and responsiveness of an on demand business. With the on demand strategy, the further toward the variable end of this graph a business is, the better, because this allows the business to modify its IT services and costs as business dictates. An example of a more variable IT cost structure can be seen in the capacity on demand capabilities offered in the IBM eServer lines. As we will see in the next

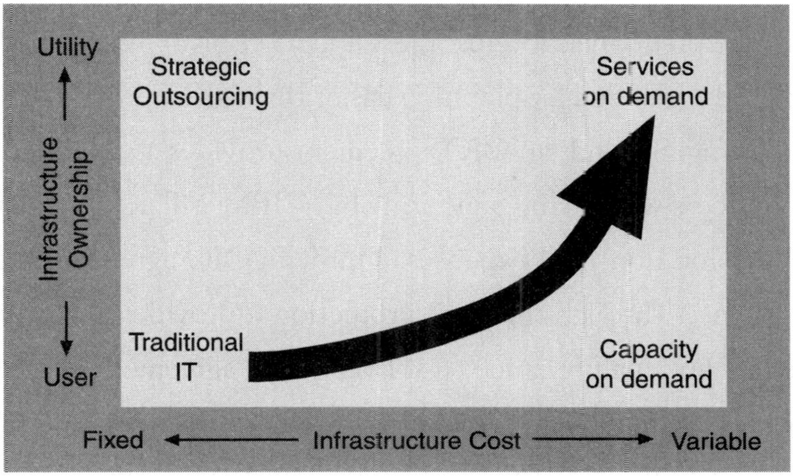

Figure 1.4. On demand leverages new ways to acquire IT resources.

chapter, capacity on demand allows a business to turn on and off extra processing power in an IBM eServer as needed—and only pay for the IT capacity actually used.

Another way to achieve a variable cost structure while using the traditional computing approach to acquiring IT assets is through the Global Financing arm of IBM. This group is focused on finding ways to help businesses build on demand operating environments with flexible cost structures through low-rate financing, leasing plans, and other special offers. For example, IBM has an Open Infrastructure Offering (OIO). This is a single, customized, and strategic agreement between IBM and a business for the acquisition of both IBM and non-IBM hardware, software, professional services, maintenance, disaster recovery, and financing. The benefits of an OIO agreement are threefold.

First, the predefined interest rates and monthly billings reduce financial risks and make budget planning easier through improved IT expense forecasting. Second, an OIO agreement provides a simplified acquisition process with a single monthly bill—IBM will act as paying agent for all IBM and non-IBM expenses. Third, an OIO agreement can reduce IT expenses through the price protection it provides against increases in software and maintenance fees. Every OIO agreement is unique and provides the flexibility to make changes in concert with changing needs. In addition to the OIO agreement, IBM Global Financing delivers a variety of leasing and TOTAL financing packages customized to meet the specific needs of a business.

The vertical axis of the graph is used to illustrate the different levels of IT ownership a business can elect. At the bottom, you see the traditional approach in which the business owns the IT assets. As you move up the vertical axis, you begin to approach a model of computing in which the business owns less and less of the IT asset it uses. At the very top of the graph you see the strategic outsourcing option in which the IT assets used by the business are owned and operated by a service company. In between these two extremes is a wide range of options that blend the two ownership models. Herein lies the new frontier of grid computing, which aims to make more efficient utilization of a collection of heterogenous IT resources. A company might choose to implement its own internal grid to maximize utilization of IT resources—an approach

MORE ON THE WEB

- IBM Global Financing offerings

(see page x)

leaning toward the "customer owned" end of the graph. Alternately, a company might choose to purchase the capacity it needs from a grid that sells IT capacity the way an electrical utility sells electricity—an approach leaning toward the "utility" end of the graph. Either way, the result is a more flexible and variable way to meet the IT needs of an on demand business model.

Linux Virtual Services is an example offering from the utility computing segment of the on demand strategy. The offering provides a way for a business to acquire large-scale Linux mainframe computing capacity (processors, storage, networking, etc.) over the Internet. Rather than having to purchase a zSeries server to run Linux applications, a business can instead opt to access a dedicated partition of an IBM owned and operated zSeries server and have IBM run the needed applications. This option eliminates the up-front capital costs of purchasing a server while also referring all the systems management efforts back to IBM. Herein lies an opportunity to consolidate server workloads (IBM will even port non-Linux applications as necessary), reduce costs, reduce headaches, gain flexibility to instantly respond to changing workloads, and only pay for the capacity you need.

For example, Mobil Travel Guide will use Linux Virtual Services to deliver its new "Mobil Companion" offering, which offers customized services to auto travelers. In this way, Mobil will only be paying for the computing power and capacity it needs rather than investing in its own physical Web, database, and application servers (see the *More on the Web* inset).

MORE ON THE WEB

- Linux Virtual Services
- Mobil Companion project
- Grid computing
- Enabling applications for grid computing with Globus

(see page x)

Linux Virtual Services is one example of IBM's growing utility computing portfolio, which also includes other managed hosting services along with industry-specific grid computing offerings and the Globus toolkit for building your own grid. All the utility computing solutions are built using the on demand operating environment products covered in the remaining chapters of this book.

The arrow in the graph depicts the trend in the on demand business model toward a more variable IT cost structure. This is achieved through a blend of owned IT resources and the utility computing approach to achieve flexibility in capacity and function at the lowest possible cost, that is, to achieve an on demand operating environment.

The Value Cycle

No matter how good a given investment may be, the funding necessary to make the investment has to come from somewhere. Figure 1.5 depicts potential sources of funding for on demand initiatives called the Value Cycle. The basic idea is to use the savings from one project to fund additional on demand initiatives. While you can enter the cycle at

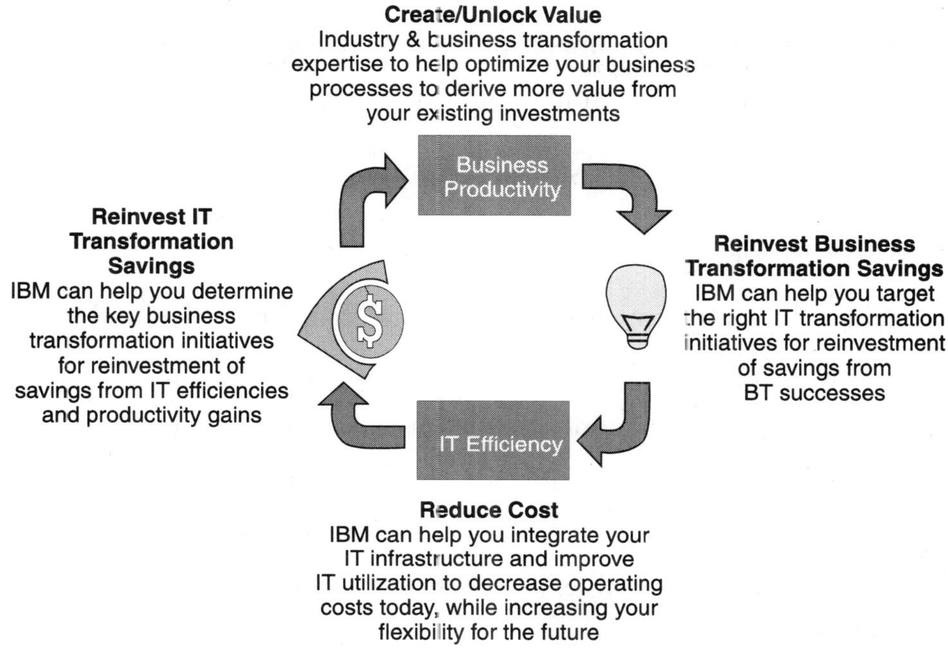

Figure 1.5. The on demand reinvestment cycle.

any point, we will begin our discussion at the "IT Efficiency" block. Often a business can do relatively simple things, such as server or storage consolidation, to reduce IT costs. The resulting "hard dollar" cost savings can then be passed up to the "Business Productivity" block, where the focus is on reducing costs through business transformation. For example, a business may choose to restructure and optimize the order-handling process. Once again, the savings from this project are then passed down to the "IT Efficiency" block, where another step down the on demand path is taken.

By starting with simpler projects that offer easily identifiable savings, you can often "jump start" your on demand journey and create cash flows that can be reinvested to keep the cycle going.

Building Blocks and Beyond

You will recall from earlier discussions that the on demand business model must be supported by a flexible computing infrastructure or "operating environment" that is integrated, open, virtualized, and autonomic. To achieve this new level of computing, there are many elements of the infrastructure that must work seamlessly together. The next two chapters will explore some of the individual elements or "building blocks" that work together to provide the basis for an on demand operating environment—namely, servers, software, storage, and printers. The last chapter will then show how some of these building blocks are combined to provide some example on demand solutions and will review IBM's roadmaps for the future of on demand.

CHAPTER 2

Server and Software Building Blocks

In this chapter, we begin our closer examination of the "operating environment" component of the on demand strategy. We will take a look at the IBM eServer product lines and some important on demand software families.

IBM eServer Systems

Underlying the e-business on demand strategy is a completely revamped line of servers that comprise the IBM eServer family. Whether a business takes the traditional path of buying IBM servers and operating their own IT infrastructure or chooses to buy IT capacity from IBM as a utility, the IBM eServer family will play a central role. Before we take a look at the different product lines that make up the eServer family, let's pause for an overall eServer strategy.

The Overall eServer Strategy

The IBM eServer product lines are designed to reduce the total cost of owning and operating an business-critical e-business computing infra-

More on the Web

- Perform your own TCO now self-assessment
- IBM eServer and on demand

(see page x)

structure (including the hardware purchase price, software licensing, installation, user training, upgrade requirements, maintenance, power consumption, facilities, systems management resources, etc.). Using eServer systems in an e-business infrastructure may help to significantly reduce total cost of ownership (TCO) over a five-year period. Lower total cost of ownership translates into greater return on e-business infrastructure investments.

According to a study of the operating e-business infrastructures of 24 organizations (Information Technology Group [(ITG]), December 2002), using eServer systems in an e-business infrastructure can help to significantly reduce total cost of ownership (TCO) over a five-year period. Lower total cost of ownership translates into greater return on e-business infrastructure investments.

IBM has achieved this lower total cost of ownership through a four-part strategy applied across all eServer products:

Application Flexibility

Freedom of choice results in lower costs. Application program flexibility offers users a wider choice of pre-packaged application programs from which to choose often resulting in lower cost application solutions. Leveraging open standards and offering more than one operating system choice (including Linux on all eServer lines) also reduces the cost of developing or integrating separate application programs. IBM eServer lines currently lead the industry when it comes to supporting both de facto and open standards.

Technology Leverage

IBM has always been and continues to be a technology innovator and leader by hiring good people, making strategic acquisitions and investments, and spending heavily on research and development. IBM has eight global research labs with over 3,000 researchers. Every year for nearly a decade now, IBM has set a new record for the most patents awarded to a single company—more than the 12 largest technology vendors combined.

Of course patents are only the beginning of the story. Technological advances only count when they are delivered in real-world products that bring tangible value to a business—another strength of IBM. Every year real-world product advancements are made at every level from microscopic packaging technologies to server and storage virtualization to global grid computing. The result is a consistent track record of improving increasing price/performance and decreasing TCO. The technological innovation engine within IBM is a key driver that helps the eServer family maintain its leadership position in the marketplace.

Risk Mitigation

The ever-present need to reduce risk drives businesses to evaluate that risk at many different levels. In the area of information technology, part of the risk profile is defined by the risk profile of the selected IT vendor:

Will they remain in business for the long term? Do they have the range of experience, products, and services that we will need for today and tomorrow? As the largest, broadest, and most experienced IT vendor on the planet, herein lies another IBM strength.

At the server level, the risk of downtime becomes a focus. To minimize the impact to business continuity resulting from downtime, IBM is taking the best ideas and technology from each eServer line and implementing them across all eServer lines.

Infrastructure Efficiency

Many of the computing infrastructure resources deployed today are underutilized. Businesses are paying for wasted performance, capacity, and human resources, thus increasing total cost of ownership. IBM is focused on enabling eServer systems to more efficiently utilize their performance and capacity with such features as "capacity on demand," which allows you to hold extra computing power in reserve that can then be quickly activated if needed (and not paid for unless activated). Another strategic technology built into many eServer systems is dynamic LPAR (logical partitioning), which allows you to partition a single eServer system such that it acts as a group of "virtual" eServer systems—each with its own users, unique characteristics, and even unique operating systems. The term "dynamic" means you can reallocate the computing resources across the partitions on the fly as needed without disrupting operations.

Common Function

As we have seen, the move towards becoming an on demand business requires migrating your IT infrastructure to an on demand operating environment model. In this section, we will examine some examples of core functions built into the eServer family to enable that migration. The examples described in this section are either fully implemented or in the process of being implemented across all IBM eServer product lines.

SMP Implementation

All IBM eServer systems support the use of multiple processors within a single system to achieve higher levels of performance. All the processors share the same memory, disk, communications adapters, tape drives, and the like (Figure 2.1). This shared memory model of computing is called symmetric multiprocessing (SMP).

The SMP implementation within IBM eServer systems enables several valuable things. First, it affords a business more choices in terms of processing power when selecting a server for a particular need. And of course it allows a business to upgrade the processing power of a server (by adding additional processors) as the business grows. Perhaps even more important, the IBM eServer implementation of SMP enables additional flexibility and another self-healing function (part of the autonomic component of an on demand operating environment).

The additional flexibility comes in the form of capacity on demand, which allows a business to switch on additional (resident but dormant)

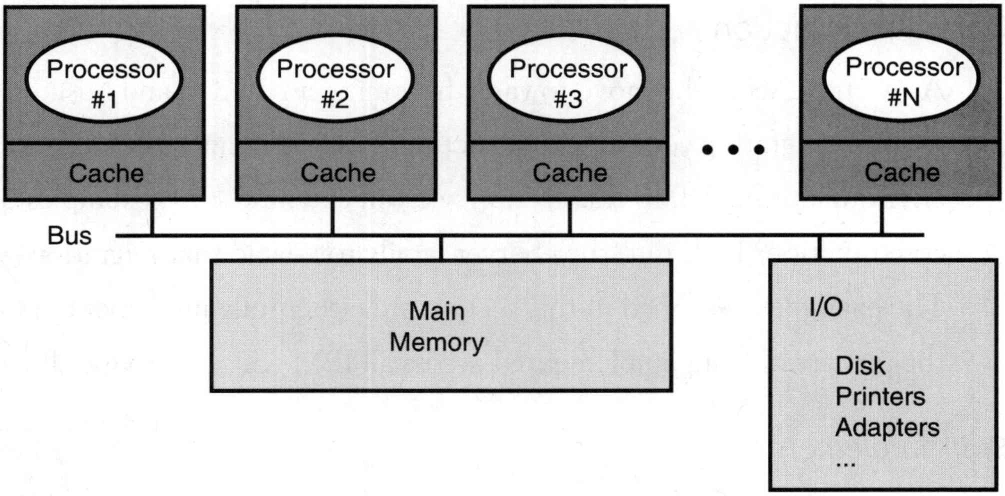

Figure 2.1. Symmetric multiprocessing (SMP).

processors as workloads increase. The new self-healing function is called dynamic processor sparing, which allows you to recover from a processor failure by activating a replacement processor (again resident but dormant). Thus, a business can quickly recover from a processor failure with no loss of processing power. The failed processor can then be repaired at some later and convenient time.

Note that SMP is not the same thing as clustering. With clusters (also supported on eServer lines), every processor in the cluster has its own memory, disk, etc., but all are cooperating closely through the high-speed connections between them. This is why clustered configurations are often called "shared nothing" configurations, while SMPs are called "shared everything" configurations.

Dynamic LPAR

LPAR refers to a popular function first introduced in IBM mainframe computers and now implemented in most IBM eServer systems. The LPAR function allows you to take a single server and make it appear to be a collection of independently operating servers. That is, you can define multiple *virtual* servers within a single *physical* server. You do this by "logically partitioning" the system into virtual servers and then allocating resources (processors, memory, input/output devices, etc.) to each virtual server. Each partition can run its own instance of the operating system, middleware, and application programs, making each an independent "virtual" server. You can even run a mix of different operating systems on a single server—each with its own partition.

Businesses can use dynamic LPAR in many ways. For one thing, you can move the workloads of multiple servers onto one partitioned server. This type of server consolidation can often yield dramatic benefits by reducing the costs associated with floor space, rack space, software licensing fees, power consumption, air conditioning, maintenance, support, etc. while simplifying systems management. Further, using the "dynamic" part of LPAR you can shift the resources from partition to partition as needed without disrupting users. You can't do this with a collection of independent servers. In short, LPAR makes for more efficient use of computing resources.

What if a problem arises in one of the partitions? There is hardware (and firmware) to prevent problems in one partition (e.g., a hardware failure or application program failure) from disrupting users in another partition.

Dynamic LPAR can be used to facilitate the testing of new application programs, new operating system versions, new devices, etc. By running a test partition you won't disrupt the real (production) users if things don't go well during the testing. This avoids the extra cost of purchasing additional independent servers for testing purposes.

Dynamic LPAR can also be employed to support backup and recovery functions, application programs that require different versions of the operating system, a fail-over backup server function, application programs requiring different time zone settings, and better utilization of scarce or expensive resources (tape libraries, high-performance communications adapters, etc.).

Capacity on Demand

Even in stable environments, it is often hard to tell what level of computing capacity one should buy for a particular situation. While it is less than ideal to buy too much capacity, it is completely unacceptable to buy too little. So most of the time you wind up purchasing more processing power and more memory/disk storage than you need, which by definition means some of that capacity is wasted.

Now factor in the unexpected—acquisitions, a current event or marketing campaign that drives masses to your Web site, etc. So to say the least, it is difficult to always purchase just the right amount of computing capacity. This problem is the genesis behind the capacity on demand function implemented in IBM eServer systems. Capacity on demand provides a way to activate additional processing power and memory and disk storage as business needs change.

While capacity on demand is implemented differently on the various eServer lines, here is how it works in general. When you order an IBM eServer system, you can get some extra standby processors and memory that lie dormant. For example, when you purchase an eServer you might get eight active processors (also called start-up processors) and eight inactive standby processors (which you don't pay for until you actually use them). If, once your eServer is installed and running, you suddenly find you need more processing power, you can activate standby processors to meet the demand. You can activate the dormant capacity under two different versions of capacity on demand: Capacity Upgrade on Demand (CUoD) or On/Off Capacity on Demand.

Capacity Upgrade on Demand is used when a business needs to permanently increase the processing power or memory of a server. Here are the steps to activating CUoD:

1. You call IBM and send them your current configuration data over the Internet.
2. IBM sends you an encrypted key over the Internet.
3. You use the key to activate the dormant processors or memory.

Nothing to install, no hardware to ship, no new contracts to sign… it's just activated and off you go. You are charged only for the additional processors and memory you choose to activate.

The other type of capacity on demand, called On/Off Capacity on Demand or On/Off CoD, is intended to meet temporary needs—that is, to accommodate peak workloads generated by such things as seasonal transaction volume increases, increased Web site traffic due to a special event, end-of-month closing cycles, etc. To use On/Off CoD, you must first enable the On/Off CoD function with a code provided by IBM. Once it is enabled, you can activate dormant processors and deactivate them as needed. The server will report processor activation, and you pay for the number of "processor days" you actually activate (less some free "processor days" IBM makes available for testing, evaluation, or special circumstances).

Another good thing about having the dormant capacity on demand processors available within a server falls in the realm of autonomic computing as described earlier. If a processor fails, a dormant processor can be activated to take the place of the failing one.

Beyond processors, IBM is beginning to deliver other IBM eServer computing resources "on demand," including memory and disk storage, as we will see later.

Linux

In addition to a primary operating system, all IBM eServer product lines now support the Linux operating system. Linux is a relatively new phenomenon in the operating systems world. It is the most successful product arising from the Open Source Initiative, which encourages programmers around the world to improve, adapt, and redistribute their software. This open source concept is gaining enormous interest as it is producing quality results in a fraction of the time required for more traditional software development.

Initially, Linux was thought of as an experimental environment rather than a serious business operating system because it lacked a warranty or guaranteed support. But now the growth of several distributors of Linux and suppliers of Linux services has helped to increase corporate support for the Linux environment. Linux has proven to be a low-cost, high-performance, secure, and highly reliable operating system. Because of this and a natural affinity for the Internet, Linux is quickly moving into the mainstream. According to the IT market intelligence firm IDC (March 2002), Linux is expected to grow at a compound growth rate of 37% between 2002 and 2005, making it the fastest-growing operating system on the planet.

IBM has fully embraced Linux and Open Source software as key components in taking e-business on demand to the next level. IBM has invested over $1 billion in Linux and has more than 7,000 employees working on Linux in research, services, development, porting centers, sales, and marketing, etc. The ibm.com Web site as well as IBM's intranet are powered by many servers running Linux. IBM is currently shipping over fifty 50 software products on Linux across its DB2, WebSphere, Lotus, and Tivoli families. Some 4,700 IBM Business Partners support Linux-enabled software. Further, IBM is working with

MORE ON THE WEB

- Introduction to Linux plus links to general Linux resources on the Web
- Open Source Initiative Web site
- History of Linux on CNN.com

(see page x)

over 250 software developers in the Open Source community to advance Linux. With this level of effort, it's no surprise that IBM was the fastest-growing Linux vendor last year.

IBM clearly believes that Linux will help enable the migration to the on demand business model by providing an open standard operating system that can harness leading-edge technologies and simplify user choice. Linux will help ensure software interoperability across heterogeneous servers.

By using the LPAR function (covered earlier), you can run one or more instances of Linux along with other operating systems on a single IBM eServer. This provides a low-risk way to test and deploy Linux application programs while simultaneously running production operating systems and their application programs.

IBM eServer Product Lines

The IBM eServer family consists of several product lines. In this section, we will take a quick look at each.

Blade Servers

The term "server blade" refers to a thin, ultra-dense card that houses microprocessors, memory, disk storage, networking, and other functions. Multiple server blades are inserted into a standardized, rack-mounted chassis—like books into a bookshelf. The chassis is equipped with interconnecting midplanes (which enable the blades to work together) and redundant components to achieve increased density, reduced electrical power requirements, higher reliability, and lower costs as compared to other servers. Emerging systems management software helps with the deployment, reprovisioning, updating, troubleshooting, etc. for local or remote configurations consisting of hundreds of blade servers. Collectively, these characteristics are making server blade configurations very popular and in keeping with the attributes of an on demand operating environment. Gartner Dataquest has forecasted that worldwide server blade shipments will grow from 84,810 in 2002 to 1 million by 2006. IDC forecasts server blade sales to reach $3.7 billion by 2006.

The server blades offered by IBM fall under the eServer BladeCenter name. BladeCenter is a broad platform that allows users to integrate and centrally manage a collection of servers, storage devices, and networking functions that collectively provide more computing power at a lower cost and in a smaller space (i.e., smaller footprint) than traditional server "box" approaches. To achieve this, BladeCenter uses a modular design packaged in high-density rack enclosures that employ Calibrated Vector Cooling techniques that enable using the more powerful microprocessors. You can quickly respond to changing workloads by repurposing existing server blades or installing additional server blades ones in a “pay as you grow” fashion.

BladeCenter is often used for server consolidation and file and printer serving, as well as e-mail, calendar, and other collaboration applications. By clustering multiple BladeCenter systems, they can also meet the needs of high-performance computing environments at a low cost. Operating system options include Microsoft Windows and Linux, which can run concurrently in a single BladeCenter using the partitioning functions provided by VMware. This enables server consolidation by allowing a business to run multiple types of workloads simultaneously.

The BladeCenter chassis is an enclosure designed to be installed in a rack and hold the server blades. Such features as redundant, hot-swappable power supplies and the redundant midplane show the focus on reliability and resiliency in the overall design at the chassis level. Figure 2.2 shows a BladeCenter chassis with installed server blades.

The BladeCenter server blades themselves also possess many characteristics that support the on demand operating environment. They implement self-healing functions such as DDR, ECC, and Chipkill memory functions; Predictive Failure Analysis; and RAID (redundant array of inexpensive disks) disk configurations that improve system reliability and availability at the blade level. In addition,

Figure 2.2. IBM eServer BladeCenter.

the disk drives, processors, blowers, and memory are covered by the predictive failure analysis function. Also, Light Path Diagnostics are used to visually guide you to failed components thus reducing repair time. The "call home" function will automatically contact IBM in the event of a failure.

Part of the server blade's computing power is used to implement other workload management and virtualization functions. There is also a dedicated system management processor that, along with IBM Director systems management software, allows you to manage one or more BladeCenter chassis and the many other elements of an integrated computing infrastructure through a single console. You can do things like update, troubleshoot, deploy, or re-provision BladeCenter resources. IBM Director also provides support for multiple clients including Linux clients for heterogeneous environments. For additional systems management capabilities, you can add the IBM Director Server Plus Pack option.

MORE ON THE WEB

- BladeCenter virtual tour
- BladeCenter video
- BladeCenter introduction and links

(see page x)

BladeCenter supports the attachment of remote storage devices through low-cost network-attached storage (NAS) devices and high-performance storage area networks (SAN) offerings. NAS devices are attached through the Gigabit Ethernet connections while SANs use Fibre Channel connections. The IBM TotalStorage NAS and FAStT families of storage products are supported by BladeCenter, allowing for the construction of an integrated infrastructure of processors, storage, and networking.

Collectively, the design features of the BladeCenter Chassis, associated components, the server blades themselves, and the supporting software help BladeCenter configurations meet the autonomic requirements of an on demand operating environment for self-configuring, self-healing, and self-optimizing, and self protecting.

Additional blade servers, such as a POWER blade (based on pSeries technology) and a storage networking blade, are in development. IBM also plans to offer a form of capacity on demand BladeCenter configuration which that would come with some extra server blades installed but not activated. You could then choose to pay for and activate the extra blades only if needed.

zSeries

IBM eServer zSeries is the mainframe server line that evolved from the S/390 world. As such, zSeries servers directly inherited all the IBM technological advances that resulted from decades of experience with mainframes in the most complex data center environments. That is, the all new design of zSeries servers builds on the security, reliability, availability, manageability, recoverability, performance, and capacity that have become synonymous with mainframe computers over the years.

The current zSeries line has also been optimized for contemporary business needs including such features as Web serving, ERP, CRM, and business continuity. As with all the eServer lines, the focus is on providing these functions at the lowest total cost of ownership. You will find zSeries servers running mission-critical business application programs at medium and large enterprises all over the world.

zSeries at a Glance

There are a range of models in the zSeries line differing in the processing power, capacity, and functions they offer. The entry-level models provide small and medium-size businesses with a server for the deployment of new e-business applications and server consolidation. From there, the zSeries models progress to increasingly powerful servers suitable for mission-critical applications for the largest enterprises. Figure 2.3 shows a zSeries server.

MORE ON THE WEB

- Printed book: *Exploring IBM eServer zSeries*
- Info on zSeries servers

(see page x)

One of the things that makes zSeries servers different from other servers is its 64-bit z/Architecture. The z/Architecture is designed to

Figure 2.3. IBM eServer zSeries.

reduce bottlenecks often created by a shortage of addressable memory through the use of 64-bit addressing. The z/Architecture, along with virtualization techniques and a focus on balanced performance across all major zSeries subsystems, allows a business to sustain higher utilization levels (averaging 70% according to IBM), making for more efficient use of IT resources. Balanced performance is achieved when all key subsystems that make up a server are well matched in terms of their individual performance levels (i.e., they can keep up with each other). Such a balanced design enables work to flow through the server smoothly and efficiently.

Another distinguishing feature of the zSeries servers is the Intelligent Resource Director (IRD). The IRD leverages virtualization, z/OS Workload Manager, logical partitioning, and Parallel Sysplex to sense workload changes in real-time and then dynamically shifts processor, memory, and I/O channel resources according to pre-defined business priorities. In this way, IRD provides the self-optimizing autonomic functions that enable a business to effectively deal with wide-ranging workload peaks and valleys.

Dynamic LPAR virtualization functions come naturally to zSeries since the concept originally came from the mainframe world. The largest zSeries servers can have up to thirty 30 partitions running a mix of different operating systems. The HiperSocket function unique to zSeries provides communications links directly between logical partitions. Conceptually, HiperSockets are virtual LANs between partitions, but since they are internal to the server, they operate at the much faster processor speeds rather than traditional network speeds. They allow

MORE ON THE WEB

- Article: *Development and Attributes of z/Architecture*
- Intelligent Resource Director

(see page x)

application programs in one partition to efficiently communicate with the application programs in others without any physical cabling—a valuable function for server consolidation and application integration projects for example.

The zSeries line uses microprocessors based on advanced chip fabrication technology and the MCM (MultiChip Module (MCM) package, which can house up to 20 microprocessors as well as cache memory and other support circuitry. The MCMs are then packaged on "books" that also contain memory and I/O channels. Spare microprocessors and memory are provided on these books for use in dynamic processor and memory sparing. Security is provided by the dedicated cryptographic coprocessors that encrypt and decrypt information in real time using Secure Socket Layer (SSL) algorithms and PIN/POS encryption.

Depending on the model, zSeries servers support both Capacity Upgrade on Demand and On/Off Capacity on Demand. With CUoD, a business can activate spare microprocessors and/or memory to gain extra processing power as needed. On/Off CoD allows a business to activate dormant processors to handle peak workloads and then deactivate them after the peak period is over. Another form of capacity on demand implemented on some zSeries models is called CBU (Capacity BackUp (CBU). With CBU, an emergency backup configuration (with additional processors

MORE ON THE WEB

- Article: *Thin Film Multichip Module Packages...*

(see page x)

activated) is defined on a designated zSeries server. In the event of a server failure elsewhere in the enterprise, the emergency configuration can be activated and use the additional processing power to temporarily take over the workload of the failed server. zSeries Workload License Charging (WLC) takes this variable computing cost notion into the software realm. With WLC, a business is charged according to the actual usage of the software. In all these cases, the purpose is to allow a business to efficiently and effectively respond to changing workloads—a necessary capability for an on demand operating environment.

zSeries servers support clustering through Parallel Sysplex configurations. With Parallel Sysplex, multiple zSeries servers (up to thirty-two 32 z/OS images) are connected through one or more Coupling Facilities. These specialized connections enable high-speed information exchange and resource sharing among all participating zSeries servers. A Sysplex Timer is used to keep the servers synchronized. Through virtualization techniques, the servers in a Parallel Sysplex provide a high-availability infrastructure with no single point of failure.

In the large enterprise, an on demand operating environment starts with the notion of an on demand data center. Such a data center is able to facilitate end-to-end enterprise integration through the adoption of open standards and the ability to change. Functions such as capacity on demand, dynamic LPAR, Parallel Sysplex, workload management,

MORE ON THE WEB

- zSeries Capacity on Demand
- Parallel Sysplex home page

(see page x)

virtualized storage, open middleware, etc. are the building blocks that can be used to build an on demand data center.

zSeries Operating Systems

The major operating systems for the zSeries include z/OS, z/OS.e, and z/VM, Linux, VSE/ESA, and TPF. Let's take a quick look at each.

In October 2000, coincident with the zSeries announcement, the new 64-bit follow-on version of OS/390 was released, named z/OS. As the premier zSeries operating system, z/OS fully exploits the 64-bit z/Architecture as well as the most advanced zSeries on demand functions. z/OS provides a highly secure, scalable, high-performance, and highly available base on which to build and deploy e-business and Java-enabled applications. The zSeries servers and the z/OS operating system preserve current investments in System/390 application programs and provide for the integration of these applications into an on demand operating environment. z/OS supports new technologies including Enterprise JavaBeans, XML, HTML, and Unicode, while supporting the technological advances in Parallel Sysplex processing and TCP/IP networking.

The Intelligent Resource Director and WorkLoad Manager (WLM) functions enable z/OS to dynamically manage resources across an LPAR. WLM can alter processor capacity, channel paths, and I/O requests across LPARs based on the business's goals and without operator intervention. This is an important evolutionary step towards an on demand operating environment and a major contributor to reducing TCO.

z/OS.e is a special limited-function version of z/OS to be used only on the z800 model for small and medium-sized businesses. z/OS.e allows businesses to deploy new application programs using zSeries and select z/OS function at a small fraction of the price of full-function z/OS implementation. An important difference between z/OS and z/OS.e is that z/OS.e will not execute CICS, IMS (Information Management System), COBOL, or FORTRAN applications. However, many precompiled COBOL, DB2, PL/1, and Visual Age PL/1 applications can be executed under z/OS.e.

MORE ON THE WEB

- z/OS operating system
- z/OS.e

(see page x)

The z/VM operating system was also a key element of the zSeries strategy. VM stands for Virtual Machine—a concept in which a single server is subdivided into multiple, virtual servers. Each of these virtual servers, simulated in software and called a virtual machine, acts as an independent and complete computer system with its own operating system image, processors, memory, I/O channels, disk storage, tape storage, etc. The operating system running in a virtual machine (on top of z/VM) is called a guest operating system and might be z/OS, z/OS.e, OS/390, VSE/ESA, TPF, VM/ESA, zVM, or Linux. The virtualization functions provided by z/VM play right into the hands of an on demand operating environment.

z/VM exploits the new 64-bit z/Architecture, thereby reducing storage constraints and giving users the significant "headroom" needed to accommodate growing e-business application program demands.

MORE ON THE WEB

- z/VM operating system

(see page x)

z/VM provides a flexible test and production environment for zSeries servers.

In December of 1999 IBM shocked the industry when it distributed Linux enhancements to allow Linux to run on IBM mainframe computers. Since then, Linux has become an important operating system for all eServer lines. Current Linux releases take advantage of zSeries hardware and the 64-bit z/Architecture. By running Linux on zSeries, a business has an on demand operating environment platform that is massively scalable both vertically and horizontally. For example, you can run hundreds of Linux images on a single zSeries under z/VM to support large server consolidation projects. When Linux is the guest operating system running under z/VM, additional benefits accrue through the ability to share hardware and software resources and use high-speed communications. Another advantage of running Linux on zSeries is that Linux application programs have access to enterprise data and application programs, facilitating end-to-end enterprise integration efforts.

In order to accommodate favorable pricing models, Linux is run on specific and dedicated processors within a zSeries server which can not be used for other workloads. The Integrated Facility for Linux (IFL) feature provides a way to add processing capacity exclusively used for Linux workloads. This permits new Linux workload running on IFL microprocessors to be added without affecting zSeries model designation or software charges for other workloads.

MORE ON THE WEB

- Linux for zSeries

(see page x)

The Virtual Storage Extended/Enterprise System Architecture (VSE/ESA) operating system is used primarily in small to mid-sized zSeries installations. As such, there are many VSE/ESA applications running core business functions, and there is high interest in deploying Linux applications on the same zSeries server. The latest releases of VSE/ESA have augmented the interoperability between VSE/ESA applications and Linux applications through HiperSockets. Other recent enhancements to VSE/ESA include Internet security (SSL) performance improvements as well as support for additional open standards such as SOAP and XML.

The TPF (Transaction Processing Facility) operating system is designed for businesses and organizations that have high on-line transaction volumes and large networks. Originally the result of an early 1960s project between IBM and several airlines, TPF has attracted customers throughout the world, and spread across several industries, including airlines, lodgings, banks, and financial institutions. Their common characteristic is an environment in which transaction growth is expected to be very fast or there are peak periods of intense transaction activity. TPF provides those businesses with significant competitive advantage by enabling high capacity with very low cost per transaction. TPF's high capacity and availability characteristics make it IBM's strategic, real-time High-Volume Transaction Processing platform.

MORE ON THE WEB

- VSE/ESA operating system
- TPF operating system

(see page x)

xSeries

The IBM eServer xSeries is the Intel-processor-based segment of IBM's eServer family. As with other eServer lines, the xSeries line offers a range of performance, features, functions, and packaging options (including floor-standing and rack-mounted designs). xSeries servers support several different operating systems including Microsoft Windows and Linux.

While earlier Intel-processor-based computers were PC-class systems only trusted to provide simple functions such as file and print serving, the role of xSeries servers has expanded to include critical business applications such as CRM, ERP, business intelligence, supply chain management, collaboration, etc. xSeries servers are used everywhere from small business and departmental environments to Fortune 500 companies.

MORE ON THE WEB

- Printed book: *Exploring IBM eServer xSeries*

(see page x)

xSeries at a Glance

There are many models that comprise the xSeries line. While there are some specialized systems in the line up (e.g., telecommunications servers), most can be broadly categorized in three groups: universal servers, rack-optimized servers, and high-performance scalable servers.

The "universal server" category of xSeries servers is aimed at the small business and departmental environment. They are often called upon to do file and print serving tasks or perhaps manage e-mail and other types of collaboration applications. The "rack-optimized" members of the xSeries family are designed to conserve space in a rack-mounted environment. The "high-performance scalable" xSeries category puts a premium on performance and SMP configurations in a rack-mounted package. Figure 2.4 shows some representative members of the xSeries line.

A distinguishing characteristic of xSeries servers is their Enterprise X-Architecture, which guides the incorporation of mainframe technology into industry-standard servers, namely, the xSeries line. Much of the Enterprise X-Architecture function is delivered through a chip set called XA-32 that IBM designed and now uses in some xSeries servers to coordinate the activities of key xSeries components such as microprocessors, cache, memory, I/O subsystems, etc. In large measure, this is how IBM gives xSeries servers many advanced functions that are new to the industry-standard server community yet well known by users of mainframes and other high-end servers.

MORE ON THE WEB

- More info on all xSeries server models

(see page x)

By blending the Enterprise X-Architecture with advanced Intel microprocessors, xSeries servers implement many advanced server features such as XpandOnDemand. With this function, you can start with one 4-way SMP xSeries server and later attach additional 4-way

Figure 2.4. Some IBM eServer xSeries servers, a) universal servers, b) rack-optimized servers, c) high-performance scalable servers.

SMP server nodes (through specialized high-speed SMP expansion ports) to increase capacity (more processors, memory, storage, and I/O slots) if the workload increases. Though similar to a traditional cluster in some respects, XpandOnDemand allows you to run a single operating system image across all processors and places all I/O devices (no matter which node houses them) within reach of all processors—functions unique to SMP configurations. XpandOnDemand also affords the flexibility to detach and redeploy each individual 4-way SMP server node as a stand alone server or to add SMP processors to a different xSeries server, thus balancing capacity with server workloads. This "pay as you grow" delivery of SMP computing power and flexibility in redeployment is a departure from traditional industry-standard servers and fits well into an on demand operating environment.

Another example of mainframe function is in the xSeries system partitioning, which is in the same spirit of LPAR (covered earlier) but is implemented today using physical partitioning. This allows a business to split the processing resources of a single xSeries server among up to four physical partitions, each operating simultaneously and running its own operating system image (and not necessarily the same operating system). As with LPAR, xSeries physical partitioning is useful for server consolidation, software migration, testing, version control, maintenance, workload isolation, etc. Physical partitioning is exploited by the VMware software, which provides more flexibility in partitioning an xSeries server through virtualization techniques and logical partitioning. You can expect future operating system releases to also provide more flexibility through logical partitioning functions.

Enterprise X-Architecture also enables some other enhancements, such as increased memory capacity, performance, and reliability (through Active Memory), and systems available (through Active Diagnostics), to name a few. These functions, along with such things

More on the Web

- Enterprise X-Architecture
- Virtual Tour: IBM Director software

(see page x)

as hot-swappable power supplies and integrated disk mirroring, help further improve system reliability and availability.

The IBM Director suite of software is provided on every xSeries server. This software, further described in the BladeCenter section above, works with integrated services processors to provide a set of systems management and autonomic functions such as remote tracking of xSeries server configurations and key system performance metrics.

Windows and Linux

There are several operating system alternatives available for xSeries systems including Microsoft Windows and Linux. Let's take a quick look at these two popular options.

All xSeries servers support the Microsoft Windows Server operating systems, which evolved from the Windows NT Server predecessor. The Windows Server series provide for a comprehensive Internet and user applications platform that provides gives increased reliability, availability, and scalability with enhanced end-to-end management features. At the core of Windows Server is a complete set of infrastructure services based on Microsoft's Active Directory service. The Active Directory simplifies management and provides a centralized way to manage users, groups, security services, and network resources. In addition, the Active Directory has a number of standard interfaces that make it easy to operate with a variety of applications and devices.

All xSeries servers also support the Linux operating system covered earlier. You can download Linux for the xSeries free from the Internet or buy a package of the operating system, tools, shells, and utilities such as the Java IBM Developer Kit for Linux. The IBM Developer Kit for Linux, Java Technology Edition, is a development environment for companies who want to build and deploy high-performance, Web-based server applications on Intel architecture that conform to the Java Core API. There is also the IBM Integrated Platform Express offering, which allows independent software vendors to deliver turn-key business application program solutions to their customers on a pre-integrated and tested platform consisting of xSeries, Linux, WebSphere, and DB2.

More on the Web

- Windows on xSeries
- Linux on xSeries
- Integrated Platform Express

(see page x)

There are currently over 3,500 Linux application programs enabled for Linux on xSeries supported by IBM and the IBM Business Partner network. IBM continues to work closely with the Linux Open Software community and independent software developers to maximize the exploitation by Linux of the Enterprise X-Architecture as it evolves over time.

iSeries

The IBM eServer iSeries line is designed to address the computing needs of those who run the commercial application programs found at the core of most any enterprise. That is why you find iSeries servers throughout

More on the Web

- Printed book: *Exploring IBM eServer iSeries*
- eBook: Building on Your OS/400 Investment
- eServer Magazine—iSeries edition

(see page x)

business, government, and academic organizations. They are popular with small and medium-sized businesses because their integrated operating system makes systems management easier. However, they are also popular in large business environments. In fact, IBM reports that 99 of the Fortune 100 companies and 83% of the Fortune 500 have installed iSeries servers as part of their computing infrastructures. In all these environments, iSeries servers have a very loyal following and consistently achieve the highest customer satisfaction in the industry.

iSeries at a Glance

The IBM eServer iSeries line of servers covers the range from entry servers that support modest environments all the way to high-end, datacenter-class systems previously associated only with mainframe computers. The iSeries is based on open standards. This, along with its integrated design, reliability, and support for running multiple operating systems/applications simultaneously, puts iSeries right in line with the on demand operating environment vision. Figure 2.5 shows the iSeries family.

More on the Web

- Details on all iSeries models
- Details on iSeries Editions

(see page x)

There are Standard and Enterprise Editions for most iSeries models. The Standard Edition includes the base functions and OS/400. The

Figure 2.5. IBM eServer iSeries family portrait.

Enterprise Edition includes a long list of on demand functions too numerous to list, but here are a few examples: Integrated xSeries Server, WebSphere Application Server, Lotus Sametime (100 seats), DB2 SMP, Tivoli Monitor, etc.

One of the things that makes iSeries servers different from other servers is its integrated architecture. This refers in part to the fact that OS/400 (the primary operating system for iSeries) comes pre-packaged with many software functions (database, security, workload management, etc.) that have traditionally been sold as separate products on other servers. Thus, OS/400 users are spared the effort of having to purchase, install, test, trouble shoot, and maintain independent software layers. This helps improve the return on investment (ROI) and makes iSeries systems more reliable, more capable, and easier to manage than other servers in its their class.

The integrated nature of iSeries servers also presents various opportunities for optimization not present in other systems. For example, the built-in database is integrated tightly with OS/400, the underlying iSeries machine interface, and the SMP hardware design. Among other things, this integration enables multiple processors to apply their combined processing power to a single query or to create a single database index. The result is a marked improvement in database performance.

The iSeries line uses microprocessors based on the reduced instruction set computing (RISC) concept of computer architecture. With the RISC approach, a very simple set of programming instructions is executed at extremely high speeds, resulting in better overall performance. The more powerful iSeries systems use the POWER4 microprocessor, which is the first single chip to house two processors, which gives it a significant performance advantage over competitive designs.

MORE ON THE WEB

- Collection of POWER4 technology papers produced by IBM Research
- IBM technology paper: POWER4 System Micro Architecture

(see page x)

The Dynamic Logical Partitioning (LPAR) implementation on iSeries is inherent in the iSeries architecture and provides a virtualized foundation. The largest iSeries systems can have up to 32 logical partitions. Even a uniprocessor iSeries server supports up to 10 Linux or OS/400 partitions. Each partition can support an independent set of users, yet there is only one system to manage. Resources can be reallocated to partitions dynamically without disrupting users.

MORE ON THE WEB

- iSeries LPAR—Frequently Asked Questions
- Short recap of iSeries LPAR function improvements by release
- iSeries Capacity Upgrade on Demand overview, presentations, and planning guides

(see page x)

iSeries servers implement variable processing power through both Capacity Upgrade on Demand and On/Off Capacity on Demand functions (described earlier). Today these functions are implemented for processors and IBM is evaluating the delivery of additional memory through the capacity on demand model in a future release. In both cases, capacity on demand provides flexibility that helps a business adjust to shifts in workloads without having to pay up front for extra capacity that may be seldom be needed.

OS/400 and Linux

iSeries servers have the ability to simultaneously support several different application program environments simultaneously. This is, in part, because an iSeries server can run multiple instances of three different operating systems at the same time: Operating System/400 (OS/400), Linux, and Microsoft Windows.

OS/400 implements and supports the key on demand functions within iSeries systems such as capacity on demand, dynamic LPAR, workload management, storage management, etc. OS/400 is also central to the autonomic functions of iSeries. There are self-healing functions that automate system monitoring to help prevent downtime and improve availability. There are self-optimizing functions such as dynamic storage optimization, that which automatically sees to the efficient allocation of disk space for OS/400, Windows, and Linux application programs for increased efficiency. There are graphical tools that can help automate systems management tasks. Integrated printing functions such as Advanced Function Printing (AFP) and Intelligent Printer Data Stream (IPDS) allow iSeries to produce printed output to meet varying needs.

The latest version of OS/400 is Version 5 Release 2 (V5R2). With the release of this version came new functions such as Dynamic LPAR

MORE ON THE WEB

- OS/400 V5R2 Enhancement Overview
- Application performance management—test results
- More detailed information on OS/400 V5R2 (IBM Redbook)
- Printing solutions supported by OS/400

(see page x)

for Linux, capacity on demand enhancements, an improved user interface now called the iSeries Navigator, switched disk cluster management, which improves system availability, multiple DB2 images useful for business unit consolidation, single sign-on functions through Enterprise Identity Mapping, and more.

The integrated functions of OS/400 along with its tight coupling to the underlying hardware make the iSeries line of servers unique when compared to its many single-purpose competitors.

There are also Linux applications available for iSeries servers. You can run a version of Linux directly on an iSeries server in one or more secondary logical partitions under the control of OS/400. In fact, the implementation of Linux on iSeries servers previously won "Best of Show" recognition at LinuxWorld.

Here is a quick example of how a business can use Linux on iSeries. Banco do Brasil, the first Brazilian bank to operate in domestic and international markets, was using a banking system running on iSeries servers. They decided to consolidate their European operations onto three iSeries servers in the London office: one running its core banking application programs, one dedicated to running Lotus Domino, and one running Linux. Banco do Brasil will replace a PC-based server farm with Linux on iSeries combined with six Integrated xSeries Servers. By

More on the Web

- Redbook: Linux on iSeries
- Linux for IBM eServer iSeries Web site
- Linux for iSeries offered by SuSE

(see page x)

using Linux on iSeries, the company saves on software licensing fees while gaining improved systems management functions for the xSeries servers.

By supporting so many different application program environments, iSeries servers provide users with a wider range of alternatives when searching for application programs to address various business needs as they arise. This has always been and will continue to be an important consideration when selecting servers.

Windows Integration

Since many businesses use a mix of iSeries servers and Intel-processor-based servers, IBM has developed two ways to combine their strengths, share resources, and simplify systems management.

First, there is the Integrated xSeries Server, which is basically an xSeries server packaged on a PCI card that you plug into an iSeries server. By doing so, you wind up with two types of servers (one iSeries and some number of xSeries) in the same mechanical package. In fact, you can install and manage up to 48 xSeries servers in a single iSeries server. You run OS/400 on the iSeries and Windows 2000 Server, and Windows XP, etc. on the xSeries Servers, which feature Intel Xeon processors.

The other option is to attach an external xSeries server to an iSeries via the Integrated xSeries Adapter. This adapter provides a high-speed link between an iSeries server and as many as 60 xSeries servers.

Using either approach to integrating xSeries servers with an iSeries server, several important things happen. You can centrally manage both iSeries and xSeries server operations, improving security and availability (e.g., OS/400 and Windows integrated user/password administration, storage management tasks, consolidated data backup and restore functions, etc.). You can perform these tasks from the iSeries console or in wireless environments via a Web-enabled cell phone or personal digital assistant (PDA).

This close integration between iSeries and xSeries servers also gives you the ability to treat all disk storage as one large body of storage and dynamically reallocate it (as well as other iSeries resources such as like CD-ROM drives, high-speed printers, communication links, etc.) to both iSeries and xSeries users. By using these functions to consolidate Windows servers within an iSeries server, a business can often achieve significant savings in the total cost of ownership and a more rapid return on investment.

Here is a quick example of a business that integrated its Intel-processor-based PC servers using iSeries and xSeries integration. Huhtamaki of De Soto, Kansas, is a worldwide manufacturer of packaging for leading food products. They were using AS/400 and PC servers for their enterprise resource planning systems. These servers, along with inherited systems they gained through a flurry of acquisitions, had resulted in the a proliferation of small PC servers, which brought the associated management problems, complexity, down time, and costs

More on the Web

- Study: ROI of Windows/Linux Server Consolidation on iSeries
- iSeries Windows integration info/links
- iSeries Windows integration guide
- Integrated xSeries Servers
- Sales manual pages for Integrated xSeries Adapters
- About the Huhtamaki project

(see page x)

with them. Huhtamaki decided to consolidate their operations using an iSeries 890. They used the LPAR function to accommodate the growing number of OS/400 applications. They replaced some of the small PC servers with Integrated xSeries Server cards installed in the iSeries 890. They replaced the rest of their PC servers with four IBM eServer xSeries servers attached to the iSeries 890 through Integrated xSeries Adapters. The result was significant savings in floor space, systems management costs, and tape backup time. System down time was also significantly reduced through the autonomic features of iSeries servers. This is very important, since Huhtamki estimated down time could cost as much as US $10 million per hour.

pSeries

The pSeries line is the IBM entry in the UNIX server arena with a focus on performance leadership and competitive price/performance ratios. pSeries servers are designed to address the computing needs of both high-performance computing (HPC) users and those who run more traditional commercial application programs. HPC applications can be found in business, government, and academic environments in areas such as statistical analysis, geological analysis, molecular chemistry simulations, artificial intelligence, and life sciences. Many HPC applications are best implemented on shared servers or clusters of servers, with each user accessing the cluster via a networked personal computer.

Commercial application program environments are those typically found in business, government, and academic organizations. Application programs in commercial environments cover a wide range, from general accounting and order entry to the most advanced database management systems for supply chain management, data mining, and business-to-business transactions over the Internet. In the commercial environment, sometimes there are also technical business users who, as in HPC environments, use pSeries systems for very demanding workloads such as business statistical analysis, financial analysis, economic simulations, and securities trading.

pSeries at a Glance

The IBM eServer pSeries line of servers covers the range from entry servers to high-end models and super computer-class clusters. The smallest pSeries servers

MORE ON THE WEB

- Printed book: *Exploring IBM eServer pSeries*
- eBook: Building on Your AIX Investment

(see page x)

MORE ON THE WEB

- Info on all pSeries server models
- Info on all IntelliStation models

(see page x)

are designed primarily for small to medium-sized businesses yet offer mainframe-like characteristics not typically found in entry-level UNIX servers. Larger companies may also select an entry pSeries model for situations where many small systems must be deployed in many separate locations, as in chains of retail stores. The related IntelliStation line (based on pSeries technology) provides a high-performance UNIX workstation for engineering and analysis applications.

The most powerful pSeries servers are often used in large database environments or high-performance computing markets. Figure 2.6 shows the pSeries line.

Figure 2.6. Various IBM eServer pSeries models.

As with the iSeries line, pSeries servers use RISC microprocessors that implement the IBM POWER Architecture. The most powerful microprocessor in this family is called the POWER4+, and it is used across the pSeries line.

The SMP implementation of pSeries systems allows a single server to have up to 32 processors and supports the autonomic self-healing function called dynamic processor sparing (described earlier). The memory subsystems used in all pSeries servers also employ autonomic self-healing functions such as memory deallocation, ECC Chipkill, bit steering/redundant memory, and memory soft scrubbing. These and other system-level features such as hot-pluggable PCI expansion slots, redundant power supplies and cooling fans, hot-swappable disk bays, etc. all help improve the availability of pSeries servers.

The pSeries line leverages hardware and operating system virtualization functions to implement the dynamic LPAR function. The largest pSeries systems can have up to 32 dynamic logical partitions. Each partition can run its own instance of the operating system (AIX or Linux), middleware, and application programs, making each an independent virtual server.

The latest pSeries servers implement variable processing power and memory capacity through the Capacity Upgrade on Demand and Capacity On/Off capacity on demand functions (with up to 30 free days for evaluation and testing). As discussed earlier, these functions provide variability that helps a business meet peak workload demands while only paying for the computing capacity actually activated. Of course, pSeries servers can also be scaled up in capacity either by upgrading to more powerful models or by linking (clustering) multiple pSeries systems together to achieve supercomputer performance.

More on the Web

- pSeries LPAR functions
- pSeries capacity on demand

(see page x)

AIX and Linux

pSeries servers support two operating systems: AIX and Linux. The AIX operating system is the premier operating system for pSeries servers. AIX combines the basic functions of the UNIX operating system with many enhancements, some developed by IBM and some designed by other companies and academic institutions.

AIX conforms to many open standards (e.g., Java, ISO, UDDI, SOAP, Eclipse, SET, SSL, etc.) defined by independent standards bodies. As discussed earlier, adherence to open standards is an important characteristic when building an on demand operating environment because it leads to more options when selecting application programs, easier integration of different types of computers, etc.

More on the Web

- IBM AIX Web site
- UCLA's library of public domain software for AIX
- AIX Affinity with Linux (technology paper)
- Instant Messaging for AIX (technology paper)

(see page x)

AIX implements and supports the key on demand

More on the Web

- Introduction of Linux for pSeries (technology paper)
- Linux for IBM eServer pSeries Web site
- Linux distribution for pSeries offered by SuSE

(see page x)

functions within pSeries systems like such as capacity on demand, dynamic LPAR, SMP, workload management, dynamic processor and memory deallocation, etc. AIX version 5L brings with it many enhancements, including an affinity for Linux application programs and instant messaging. There are thousands of application programs available that run on a pSeries system and AIX.

In addition to AIX, pSeries systems can also run the Linux operating system described earlier. You can choose to buy a pSeries server without an AIX license and run only Linux. Alternately, you can run one or more instances of Linux and AIX on a single pSeries server using the dynamic LPAR function. This provides a low-risk way to test and deploy Linux application programs on a pSeries server while still running production AIX application programs.

Clusters

A cluster is a collection of two or more servers interconnected via a high-speed link. The servers in a cluster combine their strengths and leverage virtualization techniques to become "one computer." Cluster-

MORE ON THE WEB

- Cluster 1600 info and links
- Cluster 1350 info and links

(see page x)

ing provides another way to scale up in computing power on demand by adding additional servers alongside existing ones, thereby preserving current investments in both hardware and software.

In addition to the zSeries Parallel Sysplex covered earlier, IBM offers two basic cluster groups: Cluster 1600 (pSeries based) and Cluster 1350 (xSeries based). These are not product lines per se, but rather the names used to refer to a related set of clustering technologies.

IBM eServer Cluster 1600 is the group that includes the AIX clustering products (pSeries servers, interconnect options, and software products). Cluster 1600 is the logical extension of the preceding RS/6000 SP technologies, which allowed hundreds of processors to be combined in massively parallel systems, such as Deep Blue (the system that defeated chess master Garry Kasparov in 1997) and ASCI White (the world's fastest supercomputer in 2000, located at Lawrence Livermore National Lab). Initially, the servers in RS/6000 SP configurations were specially designed and packaged SP nodes based on the same PowerPC and POWER architectures as those used in RS/6000 servers. Over the past few years, support emerged for attaching pSeries and RS/6000 servers as "nodes" in an SP configuration.

Recent enhancements to Cluster 1600 allow users to integrate the latest pSeries servers, existing SP nodes, xSeries servers and blades (when running Linux), and high-speed interconnect technologies in unified systems with a single point of control. You can have up to 128 nodes in a single cluster (including 32-way processors). The software used to manage the cluster can be either the Parallel System Support Programs (PSSP) or Cluster System Management (CSM) software.

Similarly, IBM eServer Cluster 1350 is the name used to refer to Linux/xSeries cluster technology. In this group, you can have up to 512 xSeries servers (1- or 2-way) participating as nodes in a single cluster. The xSeries servers must be running Linux operating system. You can use Cluster System Management for Linux or GPFS for Linux to manage a Cluster 1350 configuration.

One Size Does Not Fit All

When IBM revamped its entire line of servers under the IBM eServer brand back in October of 2000, it begged the question, "Why didn't IBM just create one line of servers rather than several lines (zSeries, iSeries, Blades, Clusters, etc.) under the IBM eServer brand?" This question is particularly relevant because IBM is using so much common function and technology across the eServer lines.

The answer is... because one size does not fit all. The wide range of environments in which computers are used today are as diverse as... well... the whole world. Computers are used everywhere from fish markets to nuclear reactors... and to manage activities from seaweed harvesting to Mars missions. Just as no single boat hull design or golf club is perfect for every situation, no one server architecture is perfect for every business environment.

In fact, even within a single enterprise it is almost always desirable to use more than one server architecture due to the wide range of needs to be filled. That's why 90% of all enterprises use multiple architectures (and 65% have three or more architectures in use). There is no one perfect architecture for every situation. By mixing and matching the various IBM eServer lines, you can take advantage of the inherent strengths of each to build a more flexible and efficient e-business infrastructure.

These, along with the need to preserve investments in the computing infrastructure in place today, are the reasons IBM chose to move several unique architectures forward into the emerging e-business world.

Software Foundations

The construction of an on demand computing environment requires a broad set of software based on open standards that provides for things like security, interoperability, systems management, application program integration, database management, collaboration, and more. IBM offers several families of software products that run across all eServer lines and provide the foundation for an on demand operating environment. In this section, we will look at four IBM software families that form the foundation bedrock of the IBM on demand strategy: WebSphere, DB2, Lotus, and Tivoli.

MORE ON THE WEB

- Printed book: *Exploring IBM e-business Software* (covers all off the core IBM software brands)

(see page x)

Tivoli

Tivoli is the arm of IBM that develops software products used to simplify the management of several key issues that arise when operating computing infrastructures. The Tivoli family includes products that help a business manage security, storage, performance, availability, configuration, and system operation.

In the area of security, Tivoli provides software that allows businesses to centrally define a security policy and have that policy consistently enforced across the entire application and server portfolio. This means that rather than doing security at an individual level, although this is still possible, individuals can be assigned to groups and automatically inherit the security rights of a group. It also means that a central, rule-based privacy/security policy can be developed. Rules can be kept in a central data store and changed in this one place as needed. Tivoli security management aids in the development and use of this policy. The Tivoli security methodology also allows the use of a single sign-on and implementation of these policies across heterogeneous systems.

In the area of storage management, Tivoli again offers an array of products such as the IBM Tivoli Storage Manager. Many of these allow you to manage the multiple terabytes and petabytes of data acquired from Web contacts and nontraditional media, such as voice and pictures. Some of these solutions also help you back up and recover data, including the tools necessary to gain off-site recovery. As the volume of information explodes, the task of managing that

MORE ON THE WEB

- Tivoli Software information

(see page x)

information and insuring its availability becomes too big to manage manually. Tivoli offers a comprehensive SAN (Storage Area Network) solutions that provides end-to-end data protection, resource sharing, and SAN management for complex storage environments.

Tivoli also offers a set of software products that address the management of system performance and availability. This software monitors the different components of a business's computing infrastructure. Based on policy set up, the products can send an alert, perform an action, or, in some cases, analyze, determine, and act on the information it receives without human intervention. This is indicative of the self-healing and self-optimizing software functions that arise from the autonomic computing element of an on demand operating environment.

Configuring and operating computing infrastructures is becoming an increasingly complex undertaking. As a business progresses down the on demand path, complexity will increase, and this is the impetus behind the autonomic computing initiative described earlier. Tivoli offers a line of configuration and operations software designed to provide the self-configuring and self-optimizing, tools that help reduce these complexities. For example, Tivoli Configuration Manager provides the software to effectively manage software distribution over servers, desktops, laptops, and other multiple devices, including pervasive devices such as Palm OS, PocketPC, and Nokia Communicator devices. The Tivoli configuration and operations management solutions are integrated products that can be purchased as a suite to provide an integrated result to help a business reduce costs, gain automated control of a computing infrastructure, and improve organization productivity.

WebSphere

WebSphere is a family of IBM software products that provide an open standard platform and tools that help a business develop, deploy, and integrate e-business application programs. The family is composed of many components that are loosely categorized into four groups: Foundation & Tools, Business Portals, Business Integration, and Transaction Servers & Tools.

The Foundation & Tools segment of the WebSphere family contains the core components of the WebSphere architecture. These include products that prepare existing applications for e-business on demand. Following a component structure, applications are integrated into automated, connected processes. The foundation of the WebSphere Software Platform is WebSphere Application Server. This middleware component provides the functions required to receive requests, execute functions, and interface with all other WebSphere components. It also provides a runtime environment for J2EE and Web services application programs, and allows them to access data from relational databases, legacy systems such as CICS (Customer Information Control System) and IMS (Information Management System), other application servers such as Lotus Domino, and CRM or ERP systems. This enables a business to integrate existing business processes with new Web applications using Web services, with little understanding of the old technology required.

The Business Portals segment of the WebSphere family includes the software components that allow you to create and customize the interface your customers use to interact with your business. These include tools that allow your users to customize their view of your Web site (personalization and portals) or access an application program from most any device (pervasive solutions, mobile connections, and voice solutions). Products in this segment include things like the WebSphere Portal and WebSphere Commerce Portal. The idea is to provide a customized interactive experience that increases the user satisfaction of a business's customers, employees, business partners, suppliers, etc.

The Business Integration segment of WebSphere includes products that help a business integrate internal and external business process workflows and integrate as well as disparate application programs. That is, business integration provides the tools to integrate data, applications programs, processes, and people. For example, the WebSphere MQ Workflow, WebSphere InterChange Server, and WebSphere Business Integration Workbench products are designed to enable business integration. This software allows you to model your enterprise business processes, cost them, simulate the processes, and then deploy them. The MQ Workflow product is also used for application program integration, enabling the flow of information between otherwise incompatible systems.

More on the Web

- WebSphere platform overview
- IBM WebSphere Web site

(see page x)

In the fourth WebSphere segment, Transaction Servers & Tools, you find software that helps you maintain and integrate your legacy systems with your current application development. This is important because there are many application programs and supporting subsystems that were originally developed many years ago that are still in productive use, often providing critical business functions. The challenge is to integrate these existing (or legacy) systems into the infrastructure as you evolve towards an on demand operating environment. The WebSphere tools a business can use to perform this integration include things like WebSphere Studio Enterprise Developer, WebSphere Asset Analyzer, WebSphere Host Integration Solution, and the CICS Transaction Gateway.

DB2

DB2 is the IBM family of database software products designed to manage large amounts of information efficiently. The software that is required to store data, move data, and manage data is in this group. Database software is already important to businesses of all sizes and will become increasingly important as a business moves towards the on demand model. The growth of information being stored is being driven fundamentally by two trends. First, the growing number of customers, employees, and business partners interacting with application programs and Web sites generates a mass of valuable business information that must be stored. Second, the type of information being stored (document images, photographs, graphics, audio, video, etc.) requires more storage space, which must be more efficiently managed. For these reasons, DB2 products are often used in conjunction with WebSphere and Tivoli software to build and manage large data warehouse projects.

The DB2 family includes the flagship DB2 Universal Database as DB2 Content Manager, DB2 Information Integrator and the U2, IMS, and Informix database products (IBM purchased Informix in 2001).

> **MORE ON THE WEB**
>
> - DB2 family info and links
> - Penn State's "Virtual Coconuts" project

(see page x)

DB2 Universal Database, IBM's relational database, is also a staple of Fortune 500 companies. In addition, IBM uses DB2 Universal Database to underpin many of its other software products, such as Content Manager and WebSphere Application Server. DB2 Content Manager and DB2 Information Integrator are primarily used for storing unstructured data such as document images, PC-created documents, photos, and videos. DB2 Everyplace makes it easy to extend DB2 database access to portable devices such as PDAs and smart phones. For example, a group of second-year Penn State University students used DB2 Universal Database and DB2 Everyplace to implement an on-line campus store called "Virtual Coconuts" as a class project. Penn State students can order Hawaiian shirts, grass skirts, and other items through Virtual Coconuts on their Palm Pilot PDAs.

IMS is a transaction-oriented database used in many everyday applications, including automated teller machines (ATMs) and travel reservation systems. Informix was acquired by IBM in 2001 because of its strong customer base in the mid-size data storage and data warehouse market. U2 is designed for use within vertical application programs.

Lotus

The Lotus Notes and Domino family of software products provides advanced communication and collaboration functions. Lotus was a key purchase for IBM in the early 1990s. With the purchase, IBM expanded into the developing collaborative world and has enjoyed great success. Lotus has continued its emphasis on collaborative products and provides the ability for global teamwork, global meetings, and global learning. Some examples of products from the Lotus family are Lotus Notes, Lotus Domino, Lotus Sametime, and Lotus Team Workplace.

Lotus Notes provides a messaging/collaboration framework based on a shared Notes database that enables geographically dispersed teams to work together efficiently. The Domino Server family is an integrated messaging and Web application software platform. It consists of several components including Domino Server (the server for Notes), Domino Everyplace (supporting wireless hand-held devices), and application program development tools such as Domino Designer, Enterprise Integrator, Domino Application Studio, etc.

MORE ON THE WEB

- Lotus family info and links

(see page x)

Lotus Sametime is a collaboration and messaging tool that provides an instant chat feature allowing people to send text messages to each other in real time. It also contains a facility to share documents during a meeting. Lotus Team Workplace is a Web-based collaborative team workspace that integrates with existing applications such as Lotus Notes, Sametime, and Microsoft Office XP. The tool helps users schedule meetings, manage tasks, communicate in real time, present ideas, and create and edit documents.

CHAPTER 3

Storage and Printer Building Blocks

So far we have surveyed the IBM servers and software components of an on demand operating environment. In this chapter, we will explore the all-important storage component of an on demand computing infrastructure. We will also take a quick look at IBM printers that can be deployed to meet the printing needs of an on demand business.

Storage

Storage devices hold the information that is the life blood of any business, and this is especially true in an on demand business. This information must be made readily available to users and application programs on various servers running various operating systems. This is necessary to ensure application availability, and to support the integration of core business processes, and to gain competitive advantage. So the same integrated, open, virtualized, and autonomic characteristics that are central to server selection are equally important when you select the storage devices and software you will use in your on demand operating environment.

The Storage Management Challenge

In the past, storage devices by themselves were considered to be just another part needed to build a server. Rarely was storage thought of as an independent and strategic tool for business. Today that has changed. As a business moves down the e-business on demand path, the amount of information to be stored grows and the dependency on that information (and thus on the storage devices that contain that information) grows stronger. The accelerating adoption of e-business on demand is therefore driving an ever-increasing demand for more storage with higher levels of availability in order to gain strategic competitive advantage. This in turn increases the costs associated with managing that information and the storage resources that hold it. Left unchecked, the storage management costs quickly dwarf other costs. In fact, IBM estimates that storage management costs can be up to 20 times the initial purchase price of the storage devices themselves. This situation has led to renewed focus on storage management software that helps IT staff deal with issues like such as information availability, backup, security, and the migration of infrequently accessed information to less expensive storage media.

IBM Tivoli Storage Manager is an important tool for addressing these growing storage management needs. It provides core functions such as data backup/restore, managed data archival and retrieval, and protection for business-critical applications. Administration across even large implementations with hundreds of computers and dozens of oper-

MORE ON THE WEB

- IBM Tivoli Storage Manager

(see page x)

ating systems is accomplished through a centralized Web-based enterprise console. Additional storage management functions are afforded through complementary products such as IBM Tivoli Storage Manager Extended Edition, IBM Tivoli Storage Manager for Storage Area Networks, Tivoli Storage Manager for Space Management, Tivoli Storage Manager for Data Protection modules, etc.

In IBM terms, hardware items—such as disk drives, storage servers, tape libraries, and storage area network switches—and supporting software are part of the IBM TotalStorage family. Here you will find storage products ranging from entry-level devices to enterprise storage systems and storage area networks. TotalStorage products support open standards defined by organizations such as the Storage Networking Industry Association (SNIA). As with servers, storage devices that employ open standards provide for more flexibility when building and evolving an on demand operating environment over time. Virtualization techniques are also used to pool storage for more effective sharing among servers and to enable hardware changes without disrupting users or application programs. Let's take a quick look at the TotalStorage product lines.

Disk Storage

The IBM TotalStorage family offers a variety of disk storage products ranging from direct-attached disk drives to complete enterprise storage systems. In this section, we will look at the TotalStorage product lines in the disk storage arena.

Midrange Disk (FAStT)

The IBM TotalStorage FAStT Storage Server family consists of midrange rack-mountable storage devices that can be used in multiple operating environments (Microsoft Windows, Netware, Linux, and UNIX). FAStT Storage Servers can be configured for autonomic self-healing data protection using RAID (levels 0, 1, 3, 5, or 10). Attachment to a host computer can be through multiple high-speed Fibre channels to allow the efficient flow of information. You can also attach FAStT Storage Servers to a SAN using a Fibre Channel switch or hub, enabling data transfers at distances of several kilometers. Figure 3.1 shows an example FAStT Storage Server.

More on the Web

- FAStT Storage Server info

(see page x)

All of the FAStT Storage Servers can be administered by the IBM FAStT Storage Manager software product. This is a network-based

Figure 3.1. FAStT Storage Server.

management tool that allows you to centrally configure, monitor, and dynamically change multiple FAStT storage servers.

Enterprise Disk (ESS)

Large-scale IT infrastructures often use the IBM TotalStorage Enterprise Storage Server, or ESS (Figure 3.2). The focus for ESS is on providing advanced performance, automation, integration, and availability functions in support of an on demand operating environment. A single

Figure 3.2. IBM Enterprise Storage Server (ESS).

ESS can house up to 384 disk drives, providing as much as 55.9 TB of high-performance, RAID-protected storage. A FlashCopy function creates "point in time" images of data stored on disk to facilitate non-disruptive backup and copy operations for data protection. Because of these capabilities, the ESS is often selected for use in environments where data is mission critical.

The ESS also features a standby capacity on demand function that helps support the variable nature of the on demand business model. For example, when a business orders an ESS with 10 "eight packs" of disk storage, an additional 6 "eight packs" are provided. The business does not pay for this additional storage capacity until it is activated. As with other forms of capacity on demand, this enables operating environments to achieve higher utilization levels without sacrificing the ability to quickly respond to changing needs.

Adherance to open standards (e.g. SMIS) allows ESS to be shared by a mix of simultaneously attached servers including both IBM eServer systems as well as many non-IBM servers. Host interfaces include Ultra-SCSI, Fibre Channel, ESCON, and FICON. ESS is designed for 24 × 7 operation, with no single point of failure. Its fault-tolerant design features include redundant power, cooling, adapters, buses, and processor complexes. Using IBM TotalStorage Expert, a network-enabled integrated storage management tool, systems administrators can analyze, manage, and

More on the Web

- Enterprise Storage Server (ESS)

(see page x)

dynamically reallocate ESS storage (and related tape library resources) among the attached servers as requirements change. This Web-based software allows users to monitor and manage the ESS from anywhere in the world using company-secured network and intranet connections.

Storage Networking

The growing importance of storage has fostered the model for storage infrastructures in which storage devices are not attached to a specific server but rather to a storage area network or SAN.

Storage Area Networks (SANs)

A SAN (Storage Area Network) or SAN is the name given to a specialized high-speed data network dedicated to storage devices. The storage resources residing in a SAN are typically shared among a group of servers attached to the SAN. A Fibre Channel Standard (FCS) type of network is often employed to provide high-speed communications medium (or "fabric") needed for a SAN (though there are some other options including Ethernet and iSCSI). SANs are best suited for situations where performance and scalability are top priorities.

More on the Web

- Paper: Demystifying Storage Networks

(see page x)

With a SAN, storage resources (disk, tape, etc.) and the information they contain can be efficiently shared, centrally managed, and protected. The benefits of a SAN include higher performance, better utilization (less wasted capacity), scalability, and reduced storage administration costs. SANs are growing in popularity because they allow a business to consolidate, virtualize, and centrally manage heterogenous storage devices.

SANs can be constructed using many different storage building blocks. A mid-range business, for example, might choose to use a FAStT700 as the core of a SAN project. A larger businesses might opt to use the Enterprise Storage Server as the foundation of a SAN implementation. Other SAN building blocks include things like the SAN switches, Fibre Channel Directors, and wiring hubs, which are all parts of a SAN's fabric. Storage management software such as IBM Tivoli Storage Manager can be used to provide additional storage management functions. Sharing of SAN resident disk storage volumes is enhanced by the Tivoli SANergy software product and the SAN Volume Controller.

MORE ON THE WEB

- TotalStorage SAN switch
- Tivoli SANergy

(see page x)

Storage Virtualization Family

The IBM TotalStorage Virtualization family of offerings is designed to simplify, centralize management, decrease downtime, and increase utilization of storage in SAN environments. Here we will cover two offerings in the Storage Virtualization family: IBM TotalStorage SAN Volume Controller and IBM TotalStorage SAN Integration Server.

MORE ON THE WEB

- Storage Virtualization family offerings

(see page x)

The SAN Volume Controller consists of a combination of hardware and software that can be integrated into an existing SAN to help simplify, gain control of, and more efficiently share storage resources. Through virtualization techniques, disparate storage devices and their controllers can be pooled into a single view to facilitate sharing among heterogenous servers, non-disruptive management, and higher utilization of storage. The result is improved utilization, reduced complexity, and lower costs associated with a SAN while preserving the existing investment in storage resources.

The SAN Integration Server is another member of the TotalStorage Virtualization family intended for situations when a business needs to implement a new SAN and wants to take advantage of the virtualization capabilities of the SAN Volume Controller. This offering is in fact a turn-key SAN that is pre-configured and installed by IBM. It consists of several products including SAN Volume Controllers, storage, and high-speed Fibre Channel switches. Either of these offerings can be augmented with additional management functions by adding Tivoli products such as Storage Resource Management, Storage Manager, or SAN Manager. Together, these offerings bring virtualization, consolidated systems management, and variability to the storage component of an on demand operaing environment.

Tape Storage

Computing systems are woven deeply into today's business processes and are at the core of day-to-day operations. The information they use is thus a valuable corporate asset that must be protected. Tape storage provides a cost-effective and efficient means of backing up and archiving the information held on disk storage. Tape storage plays a vital role in reducing storage costs, maintaining data availability in the event of hardware failures, restoring data files accidentally or maliciously erased, restoring operations after a disaster, etc. As such, tape storage is a vital part of an on demand operating environment.

IBM offers tape storage devices ranging from entry tape drives to Enterprise Tape Libraries, which can manage up to 6,240 tape cartridges full of information. In this section, we will look at some representative tape storage products.

Midrange Tape (LTO Tape Storage)

The IBM TotalStorage Ultrium Tape Library is a midrange LTO (Linear Tape—Open) tape storage product line. LTO tape is a superior alternative to DLT, 8-mm, 4-mm, or ¼ inch tape drives for streaming data applications such as backup. The LTO specification was jointly developed by IBM, Hewlett-Packard, and Seagate. The current products use the enhanced Ultrium 2 data cartridges with capacities

MORE ON THE WEB

- Animated tour of LTO storage
- LTO product family

(see page x)

of 200 GB or 400 GB compressed, but they can read and write the previous generation Ultrium cartridges. IBM's TotalStorage LTO Ultrium products are supported by the storage management software offered by Tivoli, Legato Systems, and VERITAS Software. They can participate in SAN environments and support an evolution towards an on demand operating environment. IBM reports that they have installed over 130,000 LTO tape products around the world, making them the largest tape storage provider. Figure 3.3 provides a photo of the LTO Ultrium tape family.

Enterprise Tape (3590 Tape Subsystem)

The IBM TotalStorage Enterprise Tape System 3590 is the most powerful tape subsystem offered by IBM and is intended for use in large enterprise environments. The 3590 has been quite popular, with over 100,000 installed for use with both IBM and non-IBM servers. These tape subsystems are often used for things such as Data Facility Hierarchical Storage Manager (DFSMShsm) work, master file processing, volume dumps, image storage, etc.

There are three components that together make up a 3590 subsystem: one or more tape drives, a tape controller, and a frame. By combining the variations available in each of these components, many

MORE ON THE WEB

- Enterprise Tape System 3590 details
- Enterprise Tape Library 3494 details
- Virtual Tape Server details

(see page x)

Figure 3.3. IBM TotalStorage Ultrium Tape family.

different 3590 tape subsystem configurations are possible. This flexibility allows the 3590 subsystem to meet widely varying needs. By using the IBM TotalStorage Enterprise Tape Library 3494 in conjunction with the 3590, you gain the ability to automatically handle up to 6,240 tape cartridges. You can also add the IBM TotalStorage Virtual Tape Library to increase tape processing performance and more fully utilize the storage space on each tape cartridges. Figure 3.4 shows a 3590 subsystem.

Figure 3.4. IBM TotalStorage Enterprise Tape System 3590.

Whirlpool—A Tale of Storage Consolidation

Just as a business can benefit through server consolidation, there are also significant costs savings and performance improvements are achievable through storage consolidation. Here the idea is to take a disparate and often aging set of independent storage devices and consolidate the information they contain on storage devices that can be more easily shared and managed. To illustrate the point, consider what happened at Whirlpool Corporation, headquartered in Benton Harbor, Michigan. Whirlpool, a large manufacturer of home appliances, once had a far-flung computing infrastructure with local data centers scattered around the world—each with its own servers, storage devices, application programs, networking, etc. To reduce costs and improve operations, Whirlpool consolidated the local data centers and put all corporate users on one global network. Some older in-house application programs were retired in favor of key enterprise software suites, including SAP (enterprise resource planning functions) and Siebel (supporting their customer call centers and field service operations). As part of the project, most of Whirlpool's transaction processing was consolidated into one large data center located in Benton Harbor, using four large mainframe servers and over 500 standalone UNIX (including pSeries) and Windows NT servers.

These changes resulted in significant annual savings in networking and data center costs, but Whirlpool had yet to achieve the full benefits from its consolidation efforts. They had not upgraded their aging storage infrastructure, and the response times for their SAP real-time order processing were slowing. The process of backing up the information on their old storage devices to their tape library servers was causing bottlenecks. Their overnight batch-processing window was expanding and was getting closer to interfering with daily "live" operations. In short, the storage component of their infrastructure was not up to the task. Whirlpool solved their storage problems by moving off their slow storage devices. On the mainframe side, they migrated their information from RAMAC Virtual Arrays to three large IBM TotalStorage Enterprise Storage Servers (covered below). As a result, increases in batch processing throughput ranged from 40% to 80%, and Whirlpool had their batch-processing window back under control. The upgrade to ESS

> **MORE ON THE WEB**
> - Whirlpool's e-business projects
>
> (see page x)

also improved response time for the SAP users by 21% in their Whirlpool's European operations and 25% in North America. To support the many UNIX and NT servers, Whirlpool moved away from direct-attached storage devices and implemented storage area networks, giving them the flexibility to allocate and reallocate storage as the server needs change.

According to Jim Haney, Whirlpool's VP of architecture, "Instead of giving everybody only 30% or 40% of the free disk space on a server and wasting the rest, we'll be able to optimize utilization across the storage complex." Over time, Whirlpool intends to support both mainframe and UNIX/NT servers with storage area networks and share the same storage and tape backup devices for both.

Printing Systems

Printed output is a significant part of many businesses today, yet printers remain perhaps the most under-managed asset in the IT infrastructure. Large enterprises often deploy thousands of distributed output devices and, according to Gartner Group, typically spend 1 to 3% of annual revenue on printed output (*Rightsizing Output Fleets: The Hidden Gold Mine*, Gartner Research Note, 19 March 2001). As with the other elements of an on demand computing environment, herein lies an opportunity to improve the way a business operates. That's because the same productivity enhancement, utilization, consolidation, and "total cost of ownership" concepts that are applied to the servers and storage infrastructure components are also applicable to the printing component. Companies spend millions of dollars every year on printed output, so improvements in efficiency can produce substantial savings.

While the initial purchase price of printers is always of interest, there are other factors that must be considered that directly affect TCO, including: supplies, up-time/reliability, and longevity. For example, the cost savings in supplies alone when you move from inkjet to laser printers is significant. The cost of inkjet supplies is two to three times greater than that of laser printer supplies (*Inkjet Printers Can Cost Firms More Than They Realize*", Gartner First Take, July 2002). As with servers and storage, there is also money to be saved through printer consolidation, which often results in less wasted printing resources and thus lower costs. This is especially true in distributed printing environments, where a fleet of printers is shared by users on a network.

The IBM Printing Systems division offers products ranging from simple desktop printers to large-scale "print on demand" solutions for commercial printing applications. There are printers for workgroups, for industrial environments, for high-volume cut sheet or continuous form printing, and for monochrome or color printing. Figure 3.5 shows some example printers.

IBM Printing Systems also offers a range of printing-

MORE ON THE WEB

- Info on IBM Printing Systems hardware and software
- Info on IBM Printing Systems Consulting

(see page x)

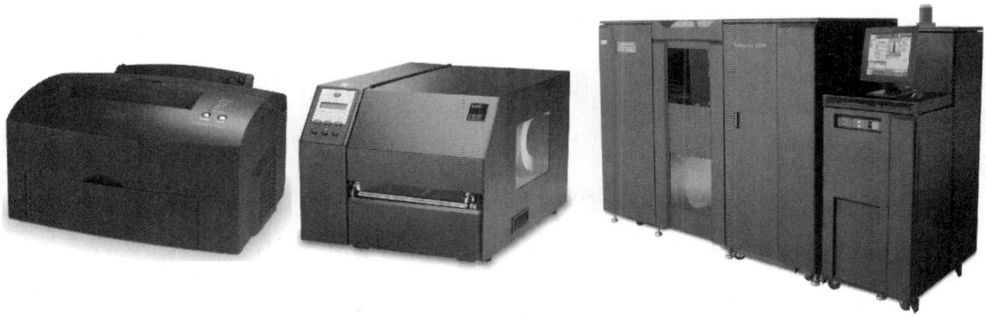

Figure 3.5. Representative IBM printers.

related software products for all IBM eServer systems. Again, the aim is to reduce the TCO for printing resources. For example, the Infoprint Manager software product provides centralized control of printing resources and autonomic computing functions. You can manage remote printers, receive notification of any printing problems, correct problems, balance printing workloads, etc. To see how Infoprint Manager can be put to work in the real world, consider the experience of Volvo Truck Corporation, who needed a more flexible printing system capable of delivering 40,000 customized technical manuals in 23 languages, "on demand" as the trucks were being built on the manufacturing line. To meet this need, print outsourcing partner Elanders upgraded to an IBM Infoprint 4100 printer and the IBM Infoprint Manager software. By doing so they were able to reduce print production lead times from several weeks to less than five hours. In on demand terms, this resulted in better customer service and an improved ability to rapidly adapt to customer needs through flexible product and process customization.

Another example of innovative printing software is the Infoprint Server, which adds integration functions to aid in the management and distribution of printed and electronic output. You can transform standard print formats directly into Web content or Portable Document Format (PDF) files for universal e-mail distribution. This is exactly what was done at E.D. Smith & Sons—a well-known Canadian manufacturer of jams and other food products. The company used Infoprint Server to re-engineer its accounts payable application and gain the ability to directly e-mail payment remittance advice (in PDF format) to its suppliers. This began a drive to electronically distribute as many business documents as possible. According to IT Director Beverly R. Russell of E.D. Smith, "Infoprint Server allows us to go to the next level of automation and reduce our distribution costs even further. By adding a few data fields that contain the recipients' e-mail addresses on to some of our master files, like our customer and vendor master, we have been able to transform our existing print/fax processes to automatically distribute these documents via e-mail at zero additional cost and have them delivered almost instantly." These are just two examples of the many printing-related software products available for a variety of eServer systems that businesses can leverage as they evolve towards an on demand operating environment.

Finally, IBM Printing Systems offers a range of printing and output-related consulting services that can help analyze your current situation and then plan and implement a printing infrastructure that enables the efficient creation and flow of printed output. These consulting services focus on finding ways to increase productivity and reduce total output costs by up to 30% according to IBM.

CHAPTER 4

Operating Environment Roadmaps and Offerings

So far we have taken a look at the broad families of servers, software, storage, and printers that provide the building blocks for creating an on demand operating environment. In this chapter, we will explore how IBM has combined these building blocks and defined a set of *Get Ready* and *Get Started Offerings* aligned with three roadmaps: Integration, Automation, and Virtualization.

Get Ready Offerings

As with any significant endeavor, time spent carefully planning each step down the on demand path is time well spent. IBM offers assistance with this planning through a set of *Get Ready Offerings* that help a business look introspectively and then compare itself with industry benchmarks. The idea is to identify and prioritize specific projects that lead down the on demand path. Some of the *Get Ready Offerings* are self-assessment tools while others are delivered by IBM Business Partners or IBM Global Services personnel.

Here are a few examples of *Get Ready Offerings*:

- **Systems IT Rationalization Study**
  A 2- to 3-week study that investigates and analyzes a business's server and storage environments and develops IBM cross-platform or platform-specific solutions and business cases for consolidation and optimization of the IT infrastructure.

- **IT Optimization Workshop**
  Two-day to two-week study focused on identifying opportunities for increasing the business value of the IT infrastructure (cost reduction, improving efficiency, etc.)

- **Storage Assessment and Research Tool (StART)**
  Tool used to evaluate alternative architectural approaches for meeting disk storage needs.

- **Autonomic Computing Value Assessment Tool**
  Tool to help a businesses assess the maturity of their existing autonomic capabilities and help guide their autonomic computing strategy.

More information on *Get Ready Offerings* are is available from IBM and IBM Business Partners.

Roadmaps and *Get Started Offerings*

Once you have a clear understanding of your current IT infrastructure situation, it's time to concentrate on specific on demand solutions available today that can move you toward an on demand operating environment. To help with this, IBM has assembled some of the on demand building blocks described in earlier chapters into a set of *Get Started Offerings*, which are available for immediate implementation.

MORE ON THE WEB

- On demand operating environment summary
- Operating environment Q&A

(see page x)

The *Get Started Offerings* are components of three distinct roadmaps: Integration, Automation, and Virtualization. Collectively, these three roadmaps embody the overall vision for on demand operating environments (Figure 4.1). By focusing on these three roadmaps and the associated *Get Started Offerings*, a business can build on existing investments and evolve in a modular and incremental way towards the on demand business ideal. Let's take a look at each area.

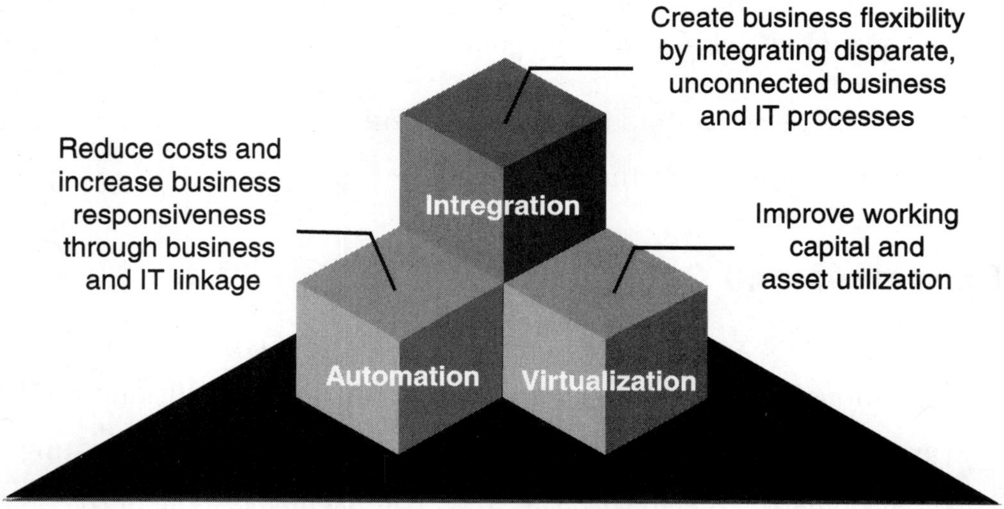

Figure 4.1. The three on demand operating environment roadmaps: Integration, Automation, and Virtualization.

Integration—Creating Flexibility

In the context of on demand, Integration is a broad term that refers to the efficient and flexible combination of resources to optimize operations across and beyond an enterprise. The idea is to bring people, processes, and information together to create a business that has the flexibility to thrive in an on demand world.

The Integration Roadmap

Figure 4.2 graphically depicts the progressive nature of integration. Starting in the lower left quadrant of this roadmap, you can see that

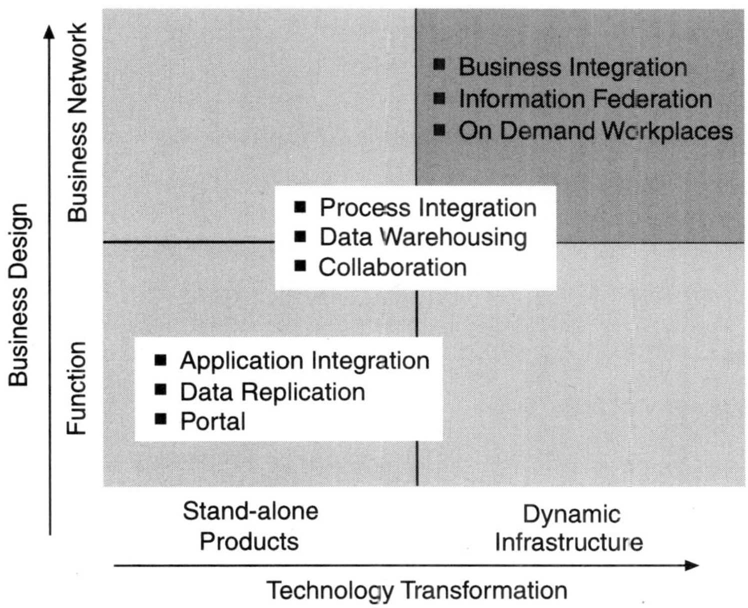

Figure 4.2. The Integration Roadmap.

early integration efforts focus on enabling the free flow of information between disparate application programs. This in turn enables the integration of the business processes they support (middle of the graph), which leads to a fully integrated business (upper right). A similar progression of integration happens with business information. Information integration may start with occasional database synchronization (data replication) and progress through data warehouse implementations and finally the "information federation" phase in which all information is brought together in one view, enabling better business decisions.

Finally, since people need to combine their efforts to create business value, enabling them to work together efficiently towards common business goals is vital. Here we are talking about enabling the collaboration of individuals and teams within a company and with key customers, suppliers, and business partners. Simple collaboration can be enabled by providing a common doorway (portal) to information, often through a Web site. More effective collaboration is provided through things like instant messaging, shared documents, on-line meetings, scheduling, virtual "team rooms," and other tools. The culmination of these collaborative functions is a complete on demand workplace where individuals and teams can productively meet, work, review, approve, and share needed information.

Get Started Offering—Business Integration

The IBM Business Integration offering is a good example for the integration offering category. This *Get Started Offering* is a series of products and methods designed to help customers progress towards the goal of end-to-end business integration. Business integration has been a goal for close to a decade, which speaks to both the importance and the difficulty of the concept. It provides the ability to integrate data, application programs, processes, and people to reduce costs and become more responsive. The result is a more competitive company that enjoys reduced business process execution costs and an enhanced ability to take advantage of new business opportunities and changing market conditions. Companies that have a high degree of business integration interact with people and groups more easily than their competitors do. This includes the ability to collaborate with supply chain partners, leverage intelligence inside the company and with external partners, and enhance customer relationship management.

The WebSphere Business Integration products allow a business to leverage past investments by integrating existing application programs, business data, and ultimately the business processes they support. Business integration requires a business process management (BPM) solution to be effective. There are several main WebSphere products to accomplish BPM. There is WebSphere Business Integration Workbench which is a set of tools that allows you to model your enterprise business processes and then efficiently test, cost, analyze, simulate, validate, and deploy those processes. There are WebSphere MQ Workflow products which support business process workflows and their interactions with people and other systems. There is WebSphere Business Integration Monitor that provides real-time information about WebSphere MQ

> **MORE ON THE WEB**
> - Integration Roadmap and *Get Started Offerings*
> - WebSphere Business Integration products

(see page x)

Workflows in process. These are just a few of the WebSphere Business Integration products in use to help a business move towards the on demand model.

See the More on the Web inset for info on other examples of *Get Started Offerings* in the integration category such as the IBM Collaboration Portal Offering.

Virtualization—Improving Utilization

The term "virtualization" refers to computer science techniques that enable efficient resource sharing, hide complexities, and provide data and application program independence from the physical details of a computing infrastructure. Through virtualization techniques, the resources within an IT infrastructure can be automatically consolidated and pooled to form a "virtual" single system illusion managed through a uniform interface. The result is an easily accessible computing infrastructure that provides more flexibility, simplified management, less wasted resource, and a lower TCO.

You may recall that virtualization is one of the four key attributes of an on demand operating environment. Earlier in this book we explored some virtualization techniques applied at the server and storage level (e. g., dynamic logical partitioning, workload management, dynamic processor deallocation, hot-swappable server blades, clustering, etc.)

that lead to better server and storage utilization. In an overall on demand context, virtualization goes beyond the substantial server and storage capabilities we have explored so far. When these capabilities are coupled with their virtualized operating systems and other enabling software technologies, you have the foundation of the on demand operating environment infrastructure.

As with other aspects of the on demand journey, the path to a virtualization and a logical rather than physical view of resources involves taking several steps. The first steps are to consolidate and simplify your server and storage resources. This lays the groundwork for pooling resources, either for an entire infrastructure or for a subset of your environment. Once this consolidation is accomplished, there are many technologies that may then be implemented to enhance and exploit a virtualized environment, including the automatic provisioning of resources such as servers, storage, networks, applications, and identities. Grid computing and Web services technologies extend the reach of the environment, not only for high-performance computing, but also for business applications. The result is an on demand operating environment offering a broader set of servers, storage, application programs, communications links, information, and even highly specialized equipment (e.g., remotely operated electron microscopes, a deep space telescope, medical equipment, etc.), still better utilization, and the opportunity for higher performance and further reductions in TCO.

The Virtualization Roadmap

Though IBM first introduced the concept decades ago, we are still just scratching the surface of the vast potential virtualization has to offer. Figure 4.3 depicts how virtualization techniques evolve up the value chain from lower left to upper right. Virtualization must necessarily begin with the server and storage building blocks that we have explored thus far (lower left quadrant of the graph). In the middle section of the roadmap, we begin to assemble these virtualized building blocks to

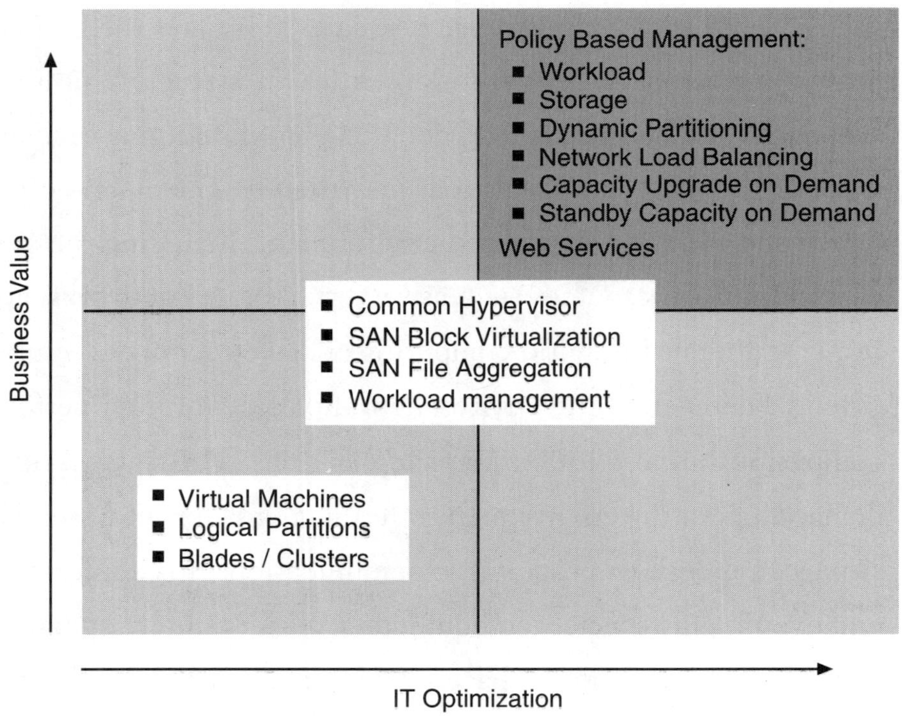

Figure 4.3. The Virtualization Roadmap.

create virtualized networks (e.g., clusters of servers, SANs, etc.). The "common hypervisor" element shown in the graph refers to a unified system management interface or conceptually the "operating system" for a virtualized network. When we get to the upper right quadrant of the roadmap, we begin to see a closer linkage between business goals and the behavior of the underlying computing infrastructure. That is, pre-defined business policies automatically dictate in real-time the capabilities and priorities of all users and resources participating in the virtualized network, helping to maximize overall business results.

Get Started Offering—Entry Virtualization Server

IBM today offers many virtualized building blocks that are used to construct on demand operating environments, including the servers, storage, and software covered earlier. IBM is also beginning to deliver virtualized on demand offerings on top of these building blocks. For example, the IBM Entry Server Virtualization offering is designed to help a business find opportunities to reduce costs, complexity, and management overhead through server consolidation. This offering consists of a *Get Ready* component and a *Get Started* component. Depending on the complexity of the environment, the *Get Ready* component may be a two- to five- day assessment process, a System IT Rationalization Study, or an IT Optimization Study (all mentioned above).

The *Get Started* component of the Entry Server Virtualization Offering consists of several building blocks including IBM eServer

More on the Web

- Virtualization Roadmap and *Get Started Offerings*

(see page x)

BladeCenter, IBM Director, and IBM Tivoli SAN manager. The ideas is to migrate the workloads off of a group of underutilized Intel servers and onto a single BladeCenter server. The benefits of doing so typically include reduced systems management complexity, improved availability, better security, better scalablity, reduced maintenance, and lower software licensing costs.

See the More on the Web inset for info on other examples of *Get Started Offerings* in the virtualization category, including the following:

- IBM TotalStorage Virtualization family
- IBM WebSphere Application Server
- IBM Grid Offering for Analytics Acceleration: Financial Markets

Automation—Increasing Responsiveness

As with integration and virtualization, automation is not new to computer systems. For decades computer systems have continually strived to become more automatic in nature, and progress has been made over time (e.g., automatic batch jobs, automatic accounting processes, and automatic backup/recovery functions). What's new is the level of infrastructure-wide automation that is required to support the emerging on demand business environment. As a business evolves towards the on demand model, the underlying operating environment necessarily becomes more complex, which drives the need for automation in all areas of the infrastructure. Without automation, infrastructures can not remain reliable, secure, affordable, or even functional.

IBM has developed the Automation Blueprint, which will guide the development of these building blocks (Figure 4.4). The bottom layer of the blueprint depicts the on demand operating environment foundation pieces (servers, storage, operating systems, middleware, etc.) upon which automation function is built. Through virtualization techniques and open standards, a business can preserve much of their current investment in hardware and software infrastructure while evolving to higher levels of automation.

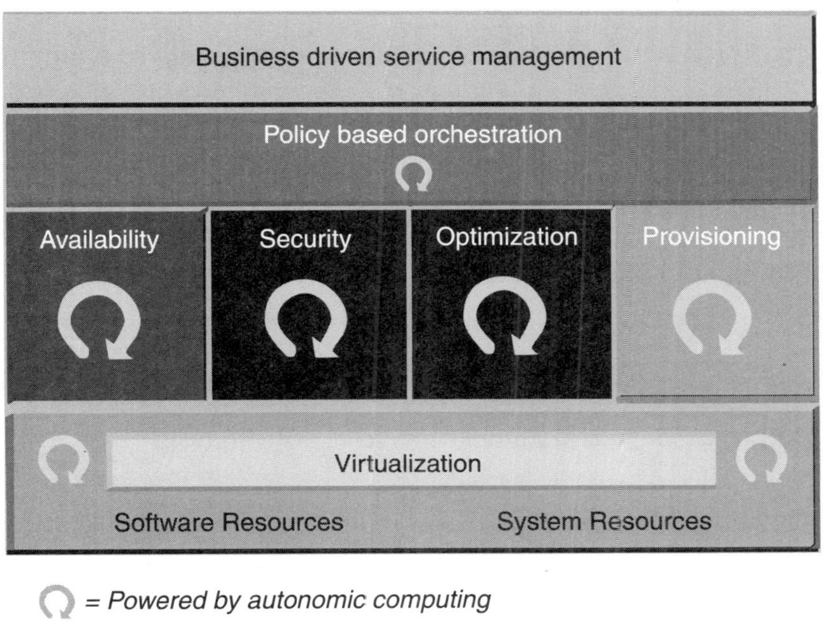

Figure 4.4. IBM Automation Blueprint.

The next layer shows where the next level of software (e.g., Tivoli, DB2, and WebSphere products) plays a key role in the areas of availability, security, optimization, and provisioning. Above that is the Policy Based Orchestration layer, which automatically dictates the response to changing infrastructure conditions according to pre-defined business policies. For this layer, IBM is combining such products as like Tivoli, WebSphere, and DB2 with some key technology gained through the recent acquisition of Think Dynamics. The top layer of the blueprint is Business Driven Service Management, where the focus is on things like billing and metering, business process modeling, service level management, etc.

You will recall from earlier discussions that autonomic computing refers to the ability to quickly "sense and respond" to changing conditions much as our own central nervous system senses and responds to change—without our conscious involvement. Increasingly automated operating environments will be achievable through the deployment of building blocks (servers, storage, software, services, etc.) that increasingly leverage autonomic computing technologies (depicted in the blueprint as a circular arrow). That is, autonomic basic functions required to achieve the highest levels of automation.

The Automation Roadmap

IBM has produced the Automation Roadmap to illustrate the evolutionary path towards higher levels of automation (Figure 4.5). The lower left quadrant of the roadmap depicts the expenses associated

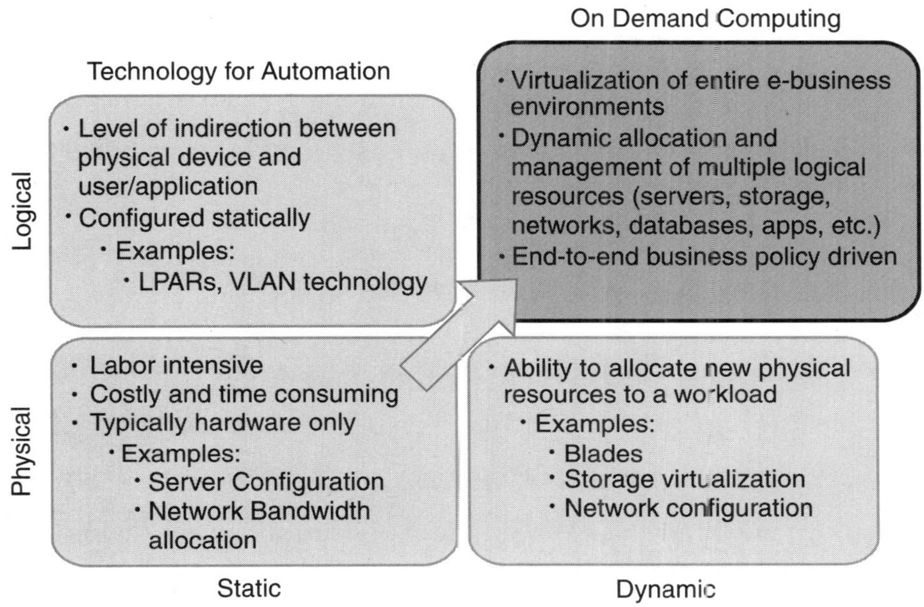

Figure 4.5. Automation Roadmap.

when only minimal levels of automation are in place—that is, when there are some system management tools in place to help with hardware-related tasks… but little else. The result is a labor-intensive environment in which people have to "micro-manage" the computing infrastructure.

As the automation level increases, things become both more logical (virtualized) and dynamic. The virtualization allows for improved utilization and simplified management of hardware and software resources—both lowering TCO. As things become more dynamic, the infrastructure is able to respond more quickly and provide higher levels of availability (e.g., preemptive problem management) and automatically shift resources as workloads fluctuate. Ultimately, we again arrive at the goal of allowing pre-defined business policies and priorities to control the automatic real-time response of an infrastructure to changing conditions.

Get Started Offering—Web Server Provisioning

IBM WebServer Provisioning is one of the *Get Started Offerings* in the automation category. It consists of a collection of hardware (IBM BladeCenter and FAStT900 storage) and software (Directory, Remote Deployment Manager, WebSphere Application Server, Tivoli's Storage Manager and Monitoring family, and DB2). This collection of on demand building blocks works together to provide a Web server that can dynamically balance workloads and self-optimize its resources to provide the best response time and system utilization. It leverages the BladeCenter's ability to shift workloads and hot-plug server blades to keep things going even in the event of various failure scenarios.

See the More on the Web inset for info on other examples of *Get Started Offerings* in the automation category including the following:

MORE ON THE WEB

- Automation Blueprint, Roadmap and *Get Started Offerings*
- Paper: Maximizing... the on demand Operating Environment
- Autonomic Assessment Tool

(see page x)

- IBM Storage Provisioning Offering
- IBM User Provisioning Offering
- IBM Availability Management Offering
- Tivoli Autonomic Monitoring Engine
- IBM Security Event Management Offering
- IBM Optimization for zSeries Offering
- IBM Optimization for iSeries Offering

The Journey Begins...

In essence, this ebook is about change and the ability to effectively respond to it. The business world is undergoing a fundamental shift which will increasingly favor the swift and nimble. Those businesses that can effectively "sense and respond" to changing business conditions will have the upper hand. IBM calls such a business an on demand business. An on demand business is responsive, variable, focused, and resilient.

The IT infrastructure that supports an on demand business must also be swift and nimble. IBM calls such an infrastructure an on demand operating environment and describes it more specifically as one that is integrated, open, virtualized, and autonomic.

In this ebook, we have briefly surveyed some key technology building blocks that you can mix and match to construct an on demand operating environment, including the IBM eServer product lines,

TotalStorage disk and tape devices, Infoprint printers, and related software. We have seen that help is available for planning and implementing a migration toward the on demand business model and the supporting on demand operating environment.

As with any major change, pursuing an on demand agenda comes with risk. You can choose not to respond to the changes taking place in today's business world, but what about your competitors? Some of them will likely choose to respond to change and in doing so find new ways to reduce their operating expenses, offer new products/services to your customers more quickly, and increase their sales at your expense. Wait until they get a foothold and it may be too late to respond in a meaningful way. So in today's world... the on demand world... the biggest risk is faced by those who choose to do nothing at all. So let the journey begin.

About the Author

Jim Hoskins is the founder of Maximum Press, a premier publisher of books, ebooks, Web content, and special reports that help businesses apply technology profitably. Mr. Hoskins has been involved with computer technology design, implementation, and education for over 21 years. He is the author of many articles, books, and ebooks covering a wide range of technology and e-business topics. Mr. Hoskins spent over a decade with IBM designing computer systems and directly helping businesses of all sizes design and implement real-world solutions. He is the author/editor of the popular *Exploring IBM* series of books, which have sold over 350,000 copies in 12 languages. Mr. Hoskins has a degree in electrical engineering from the University of Florida and resides in Gulf Breeze, Florida, with his wife and five children. You can reach him via e-mail at jimh@maxpress.com.

Appendix A: More On The Web

The best way to access the "More on the Web" links listed throughout this *MaxFacts*™ *Guidebook* is to visit the "More on the Web" section of the companion Web site. There you will find the links displayed for you and you can simply click to explore. You will find detailed directions for accessing the companion Web site on page page xi.

Alternately, you can type in the URLs for the links listed in this appendix (I would visit the companion Web site if I were you).

Page xii

- Maximum Press Web site
  http://www.maxpress.com

Page 4

- Webcast: Sam Palmisano presents on demand
  http://www.ibm.com/investor/events/ibm1002/

- On demand introductory information
  http://www-3.ibm.com/e-business/index-fl.html

- Paper: Living in an on demand world
  http://t1d.www-3.cacheibm.com/e-business/doc/content/pdf/whitepaper.pdf

Page 6

- Business Transformation Overview
  http://www-3.ibm.com/e-business/doc/content/lp/transformingbusiness.html

- IBM Business Consulting Services
  http://www-1.ibm.com/services/bcs/

- Integrated Industry Solutions
  http://www-1.ibm.com/services/strategy/industries/

Page 11

- The on demand operating environment
  http://www-1.ibm.com/servers/eserver/announce.html

- IBM autonomic computing overview, news, library, etc.
  http://www-3.ibm.com/autonomic/index.shtml

- IBM Global Services
  http://www.ibm.com/services

Page 14

- IBM Global Financing offerings
  http://www-1.ibm.com/financing/

Page 16

- Linux Virtual Services
  http://www.ibm.com/news/us/2002/07/01.html

- Mobil Companion project
  http://www.ibm.com/news/us/2002/10/042.html

- Grid computing
  http://www-1.ibm.com/grid/index.shtml

- Enabling applications for grid computing with Globus
  http://publib-b.boulder.ibm.com/Redbooks.nsf/RedbookAbstracts/sg246936.html?Open

Page 20

- Perform your own TCO now self-assessment
  http://www.ibm.com/servers/solutions/serverconsolidation/tco/

- IBM eServer and on demand
  http://www.ibm.com/eserver/ondemand

Page 30

- Introduction to Linux plus links to general Linux resources on the Web
  http://www.linux.org/info/index.html

- Open Source Initiative Web site
  http://www.opensource.org

- History of Linux on CNN.com
  http://www.cnn.com/2000/TECH/computing/02/11/mini.linux.history.idg/

Page 34

- BladeCenter virtual tour
  http://www.ibm.com/servers/eserver/bladecenter/#

- BladeCenter video
  http://www.ibm.com/servers/eserver/bladecenter/i/bladectr_svr_hmpg_hero.jpg

- BladeCenter introduction and links
  http://www.ibm.com/servers/eserver/bladecenter/#

Page 35

- Printed book: *Exploring IBM eServer zSeries*
  http://www.maxpress.com/catalog/mainframes.html

- Info on zSeries servers
  http://www.ibm.com/servers/eserver/zseries/

Page 37

- Article: *Development and Attributes of z/Architecture*
  http://researchweb.watson.ibm.com/journal/rd/464/plambeck.html

- Intelligent Resource Director
  http://www.ibm.com/servers/eserver/zseries/zos/wlm/documents/ird/ird.html

Page 38

- Article: *Thin Film Multichip Module Packages...*
  http://researchweb.watson.ibm.com/journal/rd/425/perfecto.html

Page 39

zSeries Capacity on Demand
http://www-1.ibm.com/servers/eserver/zseries/library/whitepapers/gm130257.html

- Parallel Sysplex home page
  http://ibm.com/servers/eserver/zseries/pso

Page 41

- z/OS operating system
  http://www.ibm.com/servers/eserver/zseries/zos/

- z/OS.e
  http://www-1.ibm.com/servers/eserver/zseries/zose/

Page 42

- z/VM operating system
  http://www.vm.ibm.com/

Page 43

- Linux for zSeries
  http://www-1.ibm.com/servers/eserver/zseries/os/linux/

- VSE/ESA operating system
  http://www-1.ibm.com/servers/eserver/zseries/os/vse/

- TPF operating system
  http://www.ibm.com/software/htp/tpf/

Page 44

- Printed book: *Exploring IBM eServer xSeries*
  http://www.maxpress.com/catalog/rs6000.html

Page 45

- More info on all xSeries server models
  http://www.pc.ibm.com/us/eserver/xseries/

Page 48

- Enterprise X-Architecture
  http://www.pc.ibm.com/us/eserver/xseries/xarchitecture/enterprise/index.html

- Virtual Tour: IBM Director software

  http://www-1.ibm.com/servers/eserver/xseries/systems_management

Page 49

- Windows on xSeries

  http://www.microsoft.com/windows/default.mspx

- Linux on xSeries

  http://www.ibm.com/servers/eserver/linux/xseries

- Integrated Platform Express

  http://www.ibm.com/servers/solutions/linux/integrated/xseries.html

Page 50

- Printed book: *Exploring IBM eServer iSeries*

  http://www.maxpress.com/catalog/as400.html

- eBook: *Building on Your OS/400 Investment*

  http://www.maxpress.com/ebooks

- eServer Magazine—iSeries edition

  http://www.eservercomputing.com/iseries/

- Details on all iSeries models

  http://www.ibm.com/eserver/iseries

- Details on iSeries Editions
  http://www.ibm.com/eserver/iseries/hardware/editions

Page 52

- Collection of POWER4 technology papers produced by IBM Research
  http://www.research.ibm.com/journal/rd46-1.html

- IBM technology paper: POWER4 System Micro Architecture
  http://www-1.ibm.com/servers/eserver/pseries/hardware/whitepapers/power4.html

Page 53

- iSeries LPAR—Frequently Asked Questions
  http://www-1.ibm.com/servers/eserver/iseries/lpar/lparfaq.htm

- Short recap of iSeries LPAR function improvements by release
  http://www-1.ibm.com/servers/eserver/iseries/conslt/pdf/iseries_lpar_ideabytes.pdf

- iSeries Capacity Upgrade on Demand overview, presentations, and planning guides
  http://www.ibm.com/eserver/iseries/ondemand/cod

Page 54

- OS/400 V5R2 Enhancement Overview
  http://www-1.ibm.com/servers/eserver/iseries/software/v5r2.html

- Application performance management—test results
  http://www.ibm.com/eserver/iseries/hardware/threeinone

- More detailed information on OS/400 V5R2 (IBM Redbook)
  http://www.redbooks.ibm.com/pubs/pdfs/redbooks/ga195486.pdf#page=591

- Printing solutions supported by OS/400
  http://www.printers.ibm.com/R5PSC.NSF/Web/iSeries

Page 55

- Redbook: Linux on iSeries
  http://www.redbooks.ibm.com/pubs/pdfs/redbooks/sg246232.pdf

- Linux for IBM eServer iSeries Web site
  http://www-1.ibm.com/servers/eserver/iseries/linux/

- Linux for iSeries offered by SuSE
  http://www.suse.com

Page 58

- Study: ROI of Windows/Linux Server Consolidation on iSeries
  http://www.ibm.com/eserver/iseries/conslt/idc_roi

- iSeries Windows integration info/links

http://www-1.ibm.com/servers/eserver/iseries/windowsintegration/

- iSeries Windows integration guide
  http://www-1.ibm.com/servers/eserver/iseries/windowsintegration/planguide.htm

- Integrated xSeries Servers
  http://www-1.ibm.com/servers/eserver/iseries/windowsintegration/1_6ghz.html

- Sales manual pages for Integrated xSeries Adapters
  http://www1.ibmlink.ibm.com/cgi-binmaster?request=salesmanual&parms SMS&xh=hs8UBJ3QcM1poN2USenGnN9332&xhi=salesmanual%5E&type=HARDWARE&search=integrated+xseries&title=T&product=

- About the Huhtamaki project
  http://www-3.ibm.com/software/success/cssdb.nsf/CS/LEOD-5GXSN4?OpenDocument

Page 59

- Printed book: *Exploring IBM eServer pSeries*
  http://www.maxpress.com/catalog/rs6000.html

- eBook: *Building on Your AIX Investment*
  http://www.maxpress.com/ebooks

Page 60

- Info on all pSeries server models
  http://www-132.ibm.com/content/home/store_IBMPublicUSA/en_US/eServer/pSeries/pSeries.html

- Info on all IntelliStation models
  http://www-132.ibm.com/content/home/store_IBMPublicUSA/en_US/IntelliStation_workstations.html

Page 62

- pSeries LPAR functions
  http://www-1.ibm.com/servers/eserver/pseries/lpar/

- pSeries capacity on demand
  http://www-1.ibm.com/servers/eserver/pseries/cuod/advantages.html

- IBM AIX Web site
  http://www-1.ibm.com/servers/aix/

- UCLA's library of public domain software for AIX
  http://aixpdslib.seas.ucla.edu/aixpdslib.html

- AIX Affinity with Linux (technology paper)
  http://www-1.ibm.com/servers/aix/products/aixos/linux/affinity_linux.pdf

- Instant Messaging for AIX (technology paper)
  http://www-1.ibm.com/servers/aix/os/linux/jabber/

Page 63

- Introduction of Linux for pSeries (technology paper)
  http://www.ibm.com/servers/eserver/pseries/linux/whitepapers/linux_pseries.pdf

- Linux for IBM eServer pSeries Web site
  http://www-1.ibm.com/servers/eserver/pseries/linux/

- Linux distribution for pSeries offered by SuSE
  http://www.suse.com

Page 64

- Cluster 1600 info and links
  http://www-1.ibm.com/servers/eserver/clusters/hardware/1600.html

- Cluster 1350 info and links
  http://www-1.ibm.com/servers/eserver/clusters/hardware/1350.html

Page 66

- Printed book: *Exploring IBM e-business Software* (covers all of the core IBM software brands)
  http://www.maxpress.com/catalog/ibmebus.html

Page 67

- Tivoli Software information
  http://www.ibm.com/tivoli

Page 71

- WebSphere platform overview
  http://www-3.ibm.com/software/info1/websphere/index.jsp?tab=products/platforms

- IBM WebSphere Web site
  http://www.ibm.com/websphere

Page 72

- DB2 family info and links
  http://www-3.ibm.com/software/data/database/

- Penn State's Virtual Coconuts project
  http://www-3.ibm.com/software/success/cssdb.nsf/CS/NAVO-4VPVDB?OpenDocument&Site=default

Page 73

- Lotus family info and links
  http://www-3.ibm.com/software/data/database/

Page 77

- IBM Tivoli Storage Manager

  http://www.ibm.com/software/tivoli/products/storage-mgr/

Page 78

- FAStT Storage Server info

  http://www.storage.ibm.com/disk/fastt//index.html

Page 80

- Enterprise Storage Server

  http://www.storage.ibm.com/disk/ess/index.html

Page 81

- Paper: *Demystifying Storage Networks*

  http://www.storage.ibm.com/snetwork/nas/sto_net.html

Page 82

- TotalStorage SAN switch

  http://www.storage.ibm.com/ibmsan/products/2109/san_switch_solu.html

- Tivoli SANergy

  http://www-3.ibm.com/software/tivoli/products/sanergy/

Page 83

- Storage Virtualization family offerings

  http://www.ibm.com/totalstorage/virtualization

Page 84

- Animated tour of LTO storage
  http://www.storage.ibm.com/tape/lto/lto_tour/index.html

- LTO product family
  http://www.storage.ibm.com/tape/lto/index.html

Page 85

- Enterprise Tape System 3590 details
  http://www.storage.ibm.com/tape/drives/3590/index.html

- Enterprise Tape Library 3494 details
  http://www.storage.ibm.com/tape/libraries-autoloaders/3494/index.html

- Virtual Tape Server details
  http://.storage.ibm.com/tape/libraries-autoloaders/3494-vts/info.html

Page 89

- Whirlpool's e-business projects
  http://www.ibm.com/software/success/cssdb.nsf/
  bycustomerVW?OpenView&RestrictToCategory=default-Whirlpool

Page 90

- Info on IBM Printing Systems hardware and software
  http://www.printers.ibm.com

- Info on IBM Printing Systems Consulting
  http://www.printers.ibm.com/R5PSC.NSF/Web/services+overview

Page 96

- On demand operating environment summary
  http://www-3.ibm.com/software/info/openenvironment/index.html

- Operating environment Q&A
  http://www-1.ibm.com/partnerworld/pwhome.nsf/weblook/ebusiness_QA.html

Page 100

- Integration Roadmap and Get Started Offerings
  http://www-3.ibm.com/software/info/openenvironment/integration.html

- WebSphere Business Integration products
  http://www-3.ibm.com/software/info1/websphere/index.jsp?tab=products/businessint

Page 104

- Virtualization Roadmap and Get Started Offerings
  http://www-3.ibm.com/software/info/openenvironment/virtualization.html

Page 108

- Automation Blueprint, Roadmap and *Get Started* Offerings
  http://www-3.ibm.com/software/info/openenvironment/automation.html

- Paper: *Maximizing...the on demand Operating Environment*
  ftp://ftp.software.ibm.com/software/info/openenvironment/AutoExecBrief.pdf

- Autonomic Assessment Tool
  http://www-3.ibm.com/software/tivoli/info/auto/wc_auto_tool/index.jsp?S_TACT=103A9W13&ca=tiv_web_feature

Index

Building an On Demand Computing Environment with IBM
by Jim Hoskins
152 pages
$39.95
ISBN: 1-931644-11-X

Building on Your OS/400 Investment
by Jim Hoskins
120 pages
$29.95
ISBN: 1-931644-09-8

Exploring IBM e-business Software, Second Edition
by Casey Young
360 pages
$49.95
ISBN: 1-931644-00-4

Exploring IBM Technology, Products & Services, Fifth Edition
edited by Jim Hoskins
272 pages
$54.95
ISBN: 1-885068-82-4

Exploring IBM @server pSeries, Twelfth Edition
by Jim Hoskins
and Robert Bluethman
352 pages
$54.95
ISBN: 1-931644-04-7

Exploring IBM @server iSeries, Eleventh Edition
by Jim Hoskins and
Roger Dimmick
386 pages
$54.95
ISBN: 1-885068-92-1

Exploring IBM @server zSeries and S/390 Servers, Eighth Edition
by Jim Hoskins
and Bob Frank
464 pages
$59.95
ISBN: 1-885068-91-3

Exploring IBM @server xSeries, Twelfth Edition
by Jim Hoskins, Bill
Wilson, and Ray Winkel
208 pages
$49.95
ISBN: 1-885068-83-2

To purchase a Maximum Press book, visit your local bookstore
or call 1-800-989-6733 (US/Canada) or 1-850-934-4583 (International)
online ordering available at ***www.maxpress.com***

Building on Your AIX Investment
by Jim Hoskins
104 pages
$29.95
ISBN: 1-931644-08-X

101 Ways to Promote Your Web Site, Fourth Edition
by Susan Sweeney, C.A.
528 pages
$29.95
ISBN: 1-885068-90-5

Marketing with E-mail, Third Edition
by Shannon Kinnard
352 pages
$29.95
ISBN: 1-885068-68-9

Marketing on the Internet, Sixth Edition
by Jan Zimmerman
488 pages
$34.95
ISBN: 1-885068-80-8

Business-to-Business Internet Marketing, Fourth Edition
by Barry Silverstein
432 pages
$34.95
ISBN: 1-885068-72-7

The Business Guide to Selling Through Internet Auctions
by Nancy Hix
608 pages
$29.95
ISBN: 1-885068-73-5

101 Internet Businesses You Can Start From Home
by Susan Sweeney, C.A.
520 pages
$29.95
ISBN: 1-885068-59-X

Internet Marketing for Less Than $500/Year, Second Edition
by Marcia Yudkin
352 pages
$29.95
ISBN: 1-885068-69-7

To purchase a Maximum Press book, visit your local bookstore
or call 1-800-989-6733 (US/Canada) or 1-850-934-4583 (International)
online ordering available at ***www.maxpress.com***